WITHDRAWN

Social Studies in Other Nations

Howard D. Mehlinger and Jan L. Tucker, Editors

Curriculum
Dept. of Education
Columbia College
Columbia, Missouri

BULLETIN 60
NATIONAL COUNCIL FOR THE SOCIAL STUDIES

v 300.7
M474t

NATIONAL COUNCIL FOR THE SOCIAL STUDIES

President
George G. Watson, Jr.
Winchester High School
Winchester, Massachusetts

President-Elect
Todd Clark
Constitutional Rights Foundation
Los Angeles, California

Vice-President
Theodore Kaltsounis
University of Washington
Seattle, Washington

Executive Director
Paul P. Purta
Washington, D.C.

Editor
Daniel Roselle
Washington, D.C.

Executive Secretary Emeritus
Merrill F. Hartshorn
Washington, D.C.

Directors
Daniel L. Austin
Jean Craven
William Cleveland
June V. Gilliard
Ronald G. Helms
Wilma Lund
Charles B. Myers
Richard F. Newton
Anna S. Ochoa
Arthur L. Thesenvitz
Celeste Woodley
John Rossi, *Ex Officio*

Publication Board

Carole L. Hahn, *Chairperson*
Janna M. Bremer
June V. Gilliard
Fay D. Metcalf
Karen B. Wiley
Elmer Williams
Theodore Kaltsounis, *Ex Officio*
Shirla R. McClain, *Ex Officio*

Columbia College
Columbia, Missouri

Library of Congress Catalog Number: 79-53231
ISBN 0-87986-024-3
Copyright © 1979 by the
NATIONAL COUNCIL FOR THE SOCIAL STUDIES
2030 M Street, N.W. Washington, D.C. 20036

Curriculum Resource Center
Dept. of Education
Columbia College
Columbia, Missouri

Foreword

No country, so far, has been able to reconcile the two goals of modern education; that is, to supply on the one hand some degree of cultural unity within the nation and, on the other hand, the full development of individual talent. Nor has any country solved the dilemma which stems from the twofold obligation of education; namely, to serve specific interests such as preparation for a vocation and for loyal citizenship within an individual nation, and to represent at the same time the universal values of humanity as a whole.[1]

The tension that Robert Ulich has described above is faced most dramatically by social studies practitioners. Much of the debate in the United States over the nature and purposes of social studies reflects this tension. *Social Studies in Other Nations* speaks to the universality of such concerns. Social studies educators from the Federal Republic of Germany, Thailand, Japan, Nigeria, and England have described social studies, analyzed the relationship between social studies and citizenship education, and identified the major issues in social studies in their respective countries. The editors, Howard Mehlinger and Jan Tucker, have extended the discussion, bringing the international issues into an American context. Their contribution makes explicit the value of this Bulletin for American social studies teachers. The insights gained from studying social studies in other nations may improve social studies in the United States.

Tucker specifically raises questions about the vitality of social studies in the United States compared to other nations. While "back to basics" has social studies on the defensive in the United States, Tucker observes that "With a variation in degree, the authors from other nations—Derricott, Kuhn, Meesing, Nagai, and Onyabe—view social studies in their respective nations as a force for social reconstruction." He traces this conception of social studies back to the progressive education movement in the United States and explores its tie to the global revolution of rising expectations. Then he asks the reader to contemplate whether social studies in the United States will ever regain a central role in efforts to reconstruct our society.

The National Council for the Social Studies can be justly proud of this contribution to social studies literature. I congratulate editors Mehlinger and Tucker and thank authors Annette Kuhn from the Federal Republic of Germany, Absorn Meesing from Thailand, Jiro Nagai from Japan, Vincent O. Onyabe from Nigeria, and Ray Derricott from England for essays which will engage and educate our members.

George G. Watson, Jr., *President*
National Council for the Social Studies

---

1. Robert Ulich, *Conditions of Civilized Living* (New York: E.P. Dutton & Co., Inc.), pp. 11-12.

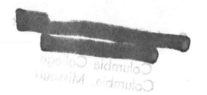

Columbia College
Columbia, Missouri

About the Authors

ANNETTE KUHN is a professor of history and methods of teaching history at the Pädagogische Hochschule Rheinland, Abteilung Bonn (Teacher Education College for Rheinland in Bonn). She is editor of the journal *Geschichtsdidaktik* and the *Journal for International Education;* and she has published books on German history and on the teaching of history.

ABSORN MEESING is employed at the National Curriculum Development Center in Bangkok, Thailand. She is one of several people who have responsibility for the development and implementation of the new social studies curriculum in Thailand. She holds a Master of Science in Education degree from Indiana University, where she studied sociology and curriculum development.

JIRO NAGAI is presently a professor of education and head, Division of Social Studies Education, Department of Education, Hiroshima University. He served as Curriculum Consultant of Area Studies at Montana State University in 1970–1971. He has been participating in UNESCO's Associated Schools Project in Education for International Understanding and Peace for the past twenty-five years.

VINCENT O. ONYABE is a lecturer in social studies education and head of primary social studies at the Institute of Education, Ahmadu Bello University, Zaria, Nigeria. He participated in the North Nigeria Teacher Education Project (NNTEP), sponsored by the Ford Foundation in 1964–1969. He was the principal of the Teacher Training College, Kaura Namoda, Nigeria in 1972 before he joined the services of the Ahmadu Bello University; and he has written several books, including social studies guides for primary school teachers.

RAY DERRICOTT is a senior lecturer in education at the School of Education, University of Liverpool, England. He is at present the director of the further development of and dissemination of Schools Council Project, History, Geography and Social Science, 8–13, which is a national development project. With his colleague Alan Blyth, he has published widely on the teaching and learning of social studies, with particular reference to children up to the age of thirteen.

HOWARD D. MEHLINGER is a professor of education and history and director of the Social Studies Development Center at Indiana University. In 1977 he was President of the National Council for the Social Studies.

JAN L. TUCKER is a professor of education at Florida International University, Miami, Florida. He served as chairperson of the NCSS International Activities Committee in 1977 and 1978. In 1977, he helped to establish an NCSS Special Interest Group, Inter-Nation Exchange for Social Studies. He chaired the NCSS Ad Hoc Committee on Global/International Education and is the current NCSS representative to the U.S. National Commission for UNESCO. His professional interests lie at the intersection of social studies, global education, and teacher training.

Preface

On Friday, November 25, 1977, a most unusual event took place at the NCSS Annual Meeting in Cincinnati. During a panel entitled "Social Studies and Citizen Education: A Multinational Approach," social studies educators from England, the Federal Republic of Germany, Japan, Nigeria, and Thailand addressed the convention theme by presenting papers on social studies in their respective countries and the relationship of social studies to citizenship education. Those attending that panel were offered a special treat: the opportunity to hear colleagues from abroad discuss issues that are at the core of social studies debate in the United States. The panel was so successful it was decided to publish its papers, thereby making them available to all NCSS members.

This Bulletin contains seven chapters. Chapters two through six are the papers presented by the foreign scholars at the NCSS Annual Meeting. Chapters one and seven were written especially for this Bulletin.

It will be helpful for the readers to know that each of the five panelists was asked to organize his or her remarks around three questions:

1. What does social studies mean in (England, the Federal Republic of Germany, Japan, Nigeria, or Thailand)?
2. What is the relationship between social studies and citizenship education?
3. What are the major issues in the social studies in (England, the Federal Republic of Germany, Japan, Nigeria, or Thailand)?

It was thought that asking each of the panelists to address these questions would facilitate comparisons among the five nations and the United States. Of course, each author was free to emphasize those aspects deemed most relevant in his or her nation.

A number of people and organizations deserve special recognition for their contributions toward making the panel and this publication possible. The NCSS International Activities Committee planned the panel together with NCSS staff and officers. John Cogan was the panel chairperson. Various groups and organizations helped meet the expenses incurred in bringing the panelists from their homes to Cincinnati. NCSS, the U.S. Department of State, the Japanese government, the Social Studies Development Center at Indiana University, and the University of Minnesota all made financial contributions in addition to the substantial investments made by the participants themselves.

We are grateful to the NCSS Publications Board for sharing our belief that the time was right for a publication on the international dimension of our own profession. We are indebted to Dan Roselle and his NCSS editorial staff for their deft touch and kind forbearance. Our own staffs deserve special thanks, including Sergei Grigoruk, graduate assistant, who read and commented on early drafts of the manuscript, and our typists Eve Russell and Donna Moriarty.

Finally, we wish to offer our own special word of appreciation to Ray Derricott, Annette Kuhn, Jiro Nagai, Vincent Onyabe, and Absorn Meesing for their important contributions to our profession. It is not an easy matter to explain complicated ideas to people of a different culture in a language other than one's own. We think they succeeded beyond all reasonable expectations.

Howard D. Mehlinger and Jan L. Tucker, *Editors*

Contents

Social Studies Education: A Transnational Profession

Howard D. Mehlinger

Social studies is spoken in many languages. Like science, music, and sports, its appeal is not constrained by culture, race, or ethnicity. No nationality owns social studies. Neither visas nor passport controls have blocked the spread of its ideas.

The transnational character of social studies education is little understood or appreciated in the United States. Although American social studies educators are among the leaders in promoting international studies and global education, although they attempt to reduce ethnocentrism and national chauvinism among their students, and even though they read about international affairs and travel widely, they are generally uninformed about their own profession as it is practiced in other nations. Even teachers who have taught in American dependents schools overseas are often ignorant of what social studies teachers do in schools immediately outside the American compound.

What accounts for this paradox? Why are American social studies teachers on the one hand eager to learn as much as they can about other parts of the world and, on the other hand, ill-informed about their own profession as it is practiced abroad?

Clearly, language is one barrier. While foreign specialists join American professional associations,[1] subscribe to our journals, and read our books, Americans are largely deprived of opportunities to follow professional discussion in other nations. Unless a foreign book or article is published in English, it will be inaccessible to most American social studies educators. Few professions suffer more from the neglect of foreign language instruction than does social studies education in the United States.

It is true that English has become the most widely used international language. It is the most popular "second language" in many nations. Since it is relatively easy to find foreign scholars who speak English, many Americans have concluded that knowing other languages is unimportant. This attitude overlooks the fact that when people write for each other, they write in their national languages and not in English. The result is that foreign scholars have access to our literature while we are prevented from reading theirs.[2]

Even when articles and books are published in English, thus making them accessible to all members of the American social studies community, they are largely ignored. Why is this true? One cannot be sure, but the answer may lie in a kind of professional ethnocentrism. The attitude of many educators seems to be: social studies is an American invention; other nations have borrowed the idea from us; they continue to learn from us; we have nothing to learn from them. Ethnocentrism is a belief that one's own group and its culture are superior to that of others. It seems that while social studies educators are eager to break down ethnocentric attitudes among their students, they may be willing to tolerate a form of it in their own profession.

Much is known about the effects of imposed isolation upon scholarship as carried out successfully by totalitarian nations. A scholarly field can atrophy or be diverted into bizarre channels. When scholars are unable to tap the worldwide community of ideas or to gain the advantage of criticism from a different cultural perspective, their intellectual growth and development are affected.

Much less is known or written about the consequences of self-imposed isolation stemming from lack of interest or unwillingness to take advantage of ideas outside of one's own group. Presumably, the results could be very similar. While individual social studies specialists have taken steps to inform themselves about practices in other countries, the profession as a whole seems to be practicing self-imposed isolation. The consequences, however serious they may be, are surely not beneficial.

Some Observations About Social Studies Worldwide

No effort will be made here to summarize social studies as it is practiced in every nation. The five chapters that follow give somewhat detailed treatments of social studies in five important nations with quite different cultural backgrounds, and at different stages of economic and political development. However, a few general observations about social studies abroad, especially as these observations are linked to social studies in the United States, could be helpful.

What Is Social Studies? One of the first problems to be faced is what kinds of courses and instruction will be counted as social studies? As Shakespeare wrote: "What's in a name? That which we call a rose by any other name would smell as sweet." To be "social studies," it need not carry that label. In Germany, it may be called political education; in England, development studies. What matters are the purposes, content, and goals of instruction.

Do courses in history and geography count as social studies? In the United States, social studies is used in at least two ways. On the one hand, it stands for a separate field of study that draws upon history, the social sciences, and other fields of knowledge for its content but combines these for purposes of helping students confront important social and personal problems. On the other hand, social studies is also used, especially in many high schools, as a kind of departmental label under which various courses are taught. As science departments offer separate courses in biology, physics, and chemistry, so social studies departments present courses in history, geography, political science, sociology, economics, anthropology, and so on.

In general—and many exceptions could be cited—foreign educators tend to accept the first meaning of social studies rather than the second. Thus "social studies," whatever term may actually be employed, is often introduced as a new course or set of courses to co-exist with (and perhaps to compete with) traditional courses in history and geography. Sometimes, social studies is seen as the edge of a more massive curriculum reform, in which social studies is introduced to replace the former curriculum that depended upon history and geography. In such cases social studies may be viewed as an interdisciplinary (or at least multidisciplinary) program with a contemporary orientation, and a focus upon perceived personal and social problems. Often social studies is interpreted as a type of citizenship (or subject) education, directed at helping socialize youth into roles appropriate to strengthen national and economic development. Social studies may or may not be linked formally to moral education, which at times exists as a separate field of study; however, it often has a strong dose of ethical training for character development.

When compared to social studies as actually practiced in the United States, in contrast to the ideological claims, social studies abroad seems to be even more interdisciplinary and problem-centered than social studies here. Other American ideas of social studies have been less fully accepted. Rote learning is still more common worldwide than inquiry teaching; social participation is seldom encouraged; instruction remains largely classroom-based. Students are expected to rely primarily upon textbooks and teachers as dependable sources of information. They are not expected to question established authorities, explore areas of interest to them, or practice their newly-acquired skills and knowledge in out-of-school settings.[3]

American teachers who hold to a less restrictive view of social studies—that is, who see social studies as a general label under which many kinds of courses can be taught—may find it useful to examine how elementary and secondary school instructors abroad teach courses in history and geography, whether the label social studies is used or not.

Social Studies: An American Symbol. Worldwide, social studies is perceived as largely an American concept. Indeed, in many nations it is either greeted enthusiastically or resisted vigorously in part because of its origin. In some of the newly independent nations, social studies has become part of the colonial debate. One reason social studies is doing well in the black African nations formerly ruled by England is that former curricular patterns are considered part of the colonial legacy. Casting aside the curriculum imposed by the English and then accepting social studies is a way of marking one's independence from the former colonial tutor.[4]

Social studies has done poorly in nations that are in some way allied against the United States. The USSR and Eastern European nations, for example, have shown little interest in utilizing American social studies ideas.

Growth of Social Studies Worldwide as a Post-1945 Phenomena. Until
World War II, there had been little interest in American social studies in
most parts of the world. Since World War II, the growth in social studies
abroad has been steady and impressive. What accounts for this growth?

Conquest is one explanation. The existence of social studies in both the
Federal Republic of Germany and Japan is a result of the American occupation policy in those nations. Occupation authorities sought to alter
schooling so as to promote democratic government and to prepare citizens for participation in it. The chapters by Professors Kuhn and Nagai
comment on this process as it occurred in Germany and Japan.

The Cold War led to another kind of American impact on other nations. Shortly after 1945, the United States began to compete with the
USSR for the hearts and minds of people residing all over the globe. One
result was the development of foreign assistance in various forms. Much
of it was military aid; some of it economic support; a smaller portion was
directed at helping developing nations build educational systems equal to
the tasks they faced.

During the 1950s and 1960s, American universities contracted with the
United States government to send educational missions to other nations.
Soon, American social studies specialists appeared in locations far-flung
over the planet. In his chapter, Vincent Onyabe discusses the impact of
such missions on the development of social studies in Nigeria.

American influence on foreign specialists has occurred both at home
and abroad. Some American scholars went overseas, and many students
from abroad came to the United States to obtain advanced degrees. Social
studies leaders abroad are often people who earned master's degrees or
doctorates in American universities, then returned to fill key educational
administrative posts. While this kind of training may have crested for
Africa, Asia, and Latin America, it is only beginning for the Middle East.
At the present time, thousands of Iranian and Arab students are pursuing advanced study in American universities. They will determine the
future of education in their respective nations.

More recently, social studies has been strengthened by the growing
worldwide concern over persistent global problems. For example, population education has grown in importance throughout the world, especially in the developing nations. Social studies is believed to provide a
more convincing rationale for population education than curricula based
upon history and geography. The African Social Studies Programme, an
organization that promotes social studies among its fourteen, English-
speaking, black African nations, has developed materials on population
for use in its member states. UNESCO's effort to encourage member nations to devote more instructional time to issues such as the "new economic order," peace, respect for other people, and human rights led to
an "International Meeting of Experts on the Role of Social Studies in
Education for Peace and Respect for Human Rights" (co-sponsored by
the National Council for the Social Studies in May, 1976), where these
and other issues were explored.

In many of the advanced, industrialized nations, social studies has
sometimes been viewed as a "soft subject," one lacking the rigor of more

disciplined study in history and geography. While this attitude has not disappeared, those holding it must increasingly cope with the demand that school instruction prepare students to deal practically with the daily problems facing society. To many individuals, social studies appears to offer greater promise for providing "relevant" instruction than do the more traditional subjects. Therefore, it seems likely that worldwide interest in social studies will grow rather than slacken in the years immediately ahead.

Why Should American Social Studies Teachers Want To Know About Social Studies in Other Nations?

A review of American social studies publications and conference presentations would reveal that a few topics dominate discourse in this field. Social studies educators are concerned primarily about classroom practice, research, theory, the linkage between classroom instruction and society, and the contributions social studies offers to citizenship development. There are undoubtedly other concerns that fall outside these categories, but the vast majority of the profession's interests fits under one or another of these labels. In each case, knowledge of social studies work in other nations could enrich social studies in the United States. Space permits the use of only a limited number of examples, but these should be sufficient to make the point.

Classroom Practice. Classroom instructional materials that can be immediately adapted for use in American schools have been developed abroad. Many of these materials are in English; thus they do not require translation. Some are on topics for which no equivalent American materials exist; others deal with topics that are treated in American books but may be handled better in foreign texts; a few are plainly more authentic.

Teachers who wish to introduce students to the subject of history and help them understand the underlying structure of this field could do no better than employ the materials termed "What is History," developed by the Schools Council History 13-16 Project in England.[5] Through a combination of booklets, evidence cards, and filmstrips, students are led to an understanding of the role of the historian as "detective," the use of historical evidence, and how one draws appropriate conclusions from such evidence. The same project has also produced an interesting paperback, *The American West 1840–1895,* that would fit easily into any high school American history course. A British perspective on the American West might add zest for American students to the study of this familiar topic.

The Institute of Education in Sierra Leone is developing the "New Programme in Social Studies" (NPSS) that will span both primary and secondary schools. This inquiry-based, multidisciplinary program is intended to foster student understanding of their surroundings, the world in which they live, and their relationships to the immediate surroundings and the wider world; to cultivate tolerance, cooperation, respect, and other socially desirable attitudes; and to teach learning and problem-solving skills. The program includes many lessons that could be incorporated within American social studies. For example, the student textbook *Man*

Himself contains a playlet written by T. Asie Lucan, entitled "Ngii Hun Gor," dealing with the problem of miscommunication and drawing upon an incident common to West Africa.

Research. Social studies research workers could profit from acquiring more information about research abroad. Often, the research topics differ from those that are popular in the United States. Occasionally, new and interesting methodologies are employed.

In England, children's historical thinking has been the focus of considerable research over the last twenty years. At least seventeen theses and many books and articles have explored this topic. In part this research has been prompted by a belief that historical thinking depends upon a different mode of thought from that employed by the social sciences, mathematics, and other fields; more recently, this research has been stimulated by the theories of Jean Piaget regarding the development of logical thinking in children. Research on history learning has been followed closely by curriculum developers in England in order to devise ways to prepare youth for historical thinking and to identify the optimum age at which to begin historical studies.[6] This research has been largely overlooked in the United States, perhaps in part because few historians have much interest in research on learning history, especially among pre-college youth; and most social studies researchers have little interest in the teaching of history at any level.

Interest in Lawrence Kohlberg's research on moral development has stimulated considerable interest in moral development and education among American social studies educators. But research on moral education and development is not exclusively an American concern. The Japanese, for example, have an Institute of Moralogy employing a full-time research staff. Their findings, some of which are reported in English, could enrich the American debate.[7]

Theory. Few questions are more likely to stir up debate among American social studies specialists than "What is the social studies?" and "Why should schools teach social studies?" In 1977, NCSS published separate bulletins that dealt with these two questions.[8] As important as these questions are, American social studies theoreticians are inclined to limit their reading to American literature and ignore relevant discussions in other nations. Indeed, American social studies educators seem isolated from the arguments that fuel controversy in other nations about the meaning and purpose of social studies.

In her chapter, Annette Kuhn refers briefly to the work of the "Frankfurter Schule," especially Jürgen Habermas and his impact on German thought regarding the desired direction for social studies. Habermas and other Neo-Marxist philosophers have been influential throughout Western Europe. Their ideas can affect how one perceives the role of the individual, the function of schools, and the relationship of both to society as a whole. Whether or not such ideas fit the American context as well or better than some other setting is not the point. There is a weakness in a profession that is incapable of appraising the assumptions and arguments held by others.

In this particular case, social studies in the United States may be suffering still from the scars of the McCarthy period. Twenty-five years ago it was dangerous for an American social studies educator to approach Marxism seriously and objectively for the purpose of learning from it. The Cold War and our antipathy toward the Soviet Union may have prevented us from remaining open to ideas that begin with a critical appraisal of society stemming from an economic analysis of its principal institutions.

Linkage Between Classroom Instruction and Society. A popular notion today is to seek ways to provide students with opportunities to participate in community life and to link classroom instruction with daily practice. Although this is not a new idea, it is enjoying a revival. It could be useful to examine programs tried in other nations. The socialist countries have been especially keen on linking the school and the community. Cuba, the USSR, and the People's Republic of China have all experimented with programs that encourage youth to contribute to their communities. Israel is another nation in which school and community life have been brought into close correspondence.

The particulars of any nation's approach may not fit United States' needs exactly. However, American educators might be provoked into fresh thinking if they were stimulated by the ideas of others.

Contribution of Social Studies to Citizenship Development

In nearly every nation social studies is seen as one of the principal vehicles for preparing youth to accept roles as "responsible adult citizens." What a "responsible adult citizen" means varies from nation to nation, but the intention is similar.

Nigeria has introduced social studies explicitly to promote citizenship development. As Vincent Onyabe's chapter makes clear, Nigeria is a geographical expression seeking to become a nation. It consists of a great many tribal, ethnic, and religious groups; the loyalty of its people has been tied traditionally to one or more of these groups and less to Nigeria as a nation. Nigeria, the largest and wealthiest black African nation, must build a sense of nationalism among its people if it is to fulfill its potential. Hand-in-hand with citizenship are the problems of economic growth and of helping young Nigerians understand how they can contribute to such development. Finally, Nigeria, presently under a military autocracy, is making the transition to democratic government. For such a government to work efficiently and justly, Nigeria will require an educated citizenry committed to democratic practices.

Nigeria is a splendid example of a new state attempting to take advantage of democratic ideals while racing toward industrialization. Social studies has been asked to carry much of the burden for teaching people what this development requires. All nations can learn from the Nigerian experience.

American projects in citizenship education, like other social studies projects during the 1960s and 1970s, have been influenced greatly by Jerome Bruner and Hilda Taba. Curriculum developers, employed by special projects, have developed new courses to serve as alternatives to those currently in the curriculum. A main feature of many of these courses is the attempt to teach students new concepts that will help them derive greater meaning from their social experience. Typically, the new concepts are technical terms borrowed from the academic disciplines. As a result, terms such as political socialization, political role, political culture, and decision-making have begun to appear in civics and American government courses.

A somewhat different kind of citizenship education reform was launched in Great Britain in 1974. In that year the Hansard Society for Parliamentary Government together with the Politics Association established the Programme for Political Education. This project had two main divisions: the curriculum development unit directed by Bernard Crick at Birkbeck College in London and the research unit headed by Ian Lister at the University of York.

The Programme's principal goal was to advance students' "political literacy," interpreted by the project staff to mean "the knowledge, skills, and attitudes needed to make a man or woman informed about politics; able to participate in public life and groups of all kinds; and to recognize and tolerate diversities of political and social values." For American citizenship educators, the project's main attraction may rest in (1) its effort to avoid the creation of entirely new courses, instead to infuse existing courses in history, geography, etc., with ideas for promoting political literacy; (2) its use of classroom teachers as developers; and (3) its dependence upon ordinary language—terms such as force, power, authority, order, law, justice, representation, freedom, welfare, natural rights, and individuality. As contrasted to American projects, the Programme avoided the introduction of specialized terminology; rather, it sought to enhance the political meaning of terms students already use as part of their daily discourse.

In all three of its major dimensions—infusion of existing courses rather than the creation of new ones, the use of teachers as developers, and dependence upon ordinary language—the Programme for Political Education provides a contrasting model for most of the citizenship education projects in the United States.[9]

What Is Being Done to "Internationalize" Social Studies in the United States?

Efforts are underway to correct the professional ethnocentrism that characterizes so much of social studies in the United States. The examples that follow are typical of such efforts.

NCSS Contributions. During the past four years, NCSS has become increasingly active in attempts to strengthen contacts with overseas experts in social studies. As noted earlier, in May, 1976, NCSS joined UNESCO in co-sponsoring an international conference on social studies. A total of fourteen social studies specialists from as many nations, plus thirty or more observers, met in East Lansing, Michigan to discuss ways that social studies could contribute to strengthening possibilities for peace and respect for other people. One result of this conference was a decision by

UNESCO to publish a *Sourcebook on the Teaching of Social Studies.* Social studies specialists from more than a dozen nations, including several people who are NCSS members, are contributors.

Two NCSS groups promote international concern within the Council. One, the International Activities Committee, is charged with the responsibility of advising the Board of Directors regarding what needs to be done in the international education field. This Committee deserves credit for bringing together the panel of foreign scholars for the 1977 Annual Meeting in Cincinnati. The papers presented on that occasion provided the impetus for this Bulletin. Currently, the International Activities Committee is preparing a directory of social studies organizations in other nations as the first step toward strengthening professional contacts with colleagues overseas. The second is a "special interest group" called "Inter-Nation Exchange for the Social Studies." This SIG was formed explicitly for the purpose of building contacts with social studies specialists abroad and of facilitating the exchange of information about social studies transnationally.

NCSS is also pursuing joint projects with other nations. One such project is an examination of history and geography textbooks used in the United States and the USSR. NCSS is one of four American professional organizations sponsoring this project; the Soviet Ministry of Education is in charge of the project for the USSR. Teams of American and Soviet scholars are reviewing selected books used in each country in order to learn what each nation teaches its youth about the other and about the relationships between the two countries. NCSS has also undertaken recent programs with Japan. In the summers of 1977 and 1978, NCSS teams of social studies educators traveled to Japan to seek ideas for strengthening American instruction about that Asian nation. During the course of their visits, the Americans had opportunities to meet Japanese social studies educators. In 1978, NCSS and Japanese authorities held discussions for the purpose of launching a joint textbook study similar to the one currently underway between the United States and the USSR.

Efforts by Other Organizations and Groups. NCSS is not alone in its desire to strengthen American understanding about social studies in other nations. A unique contribution is that offered by the Center for International Programs of the New York State Education Department. In 1966, the Center established the Educational Resources Center (ERC) in New Delhi, India, in order to provide authentic instructional materials about India for use in American classrooms. For more than a decade, American scholars and teachers have had opportunities to work at ERC. The most visible result is a growing inventory of materials about India appropriate for American classrooms. A recent example is a packet on Indian women, which contains such items as *Profiles of Indian Women* (a set of case studies about a wide variety of Indian women today) and *A World of Difference,* a more general account of the life of Indian women. While ERC has produced many excellent materials, equally important has been the opportunity ERC has afforded several hundred American teachers and scholars to meet Indian scholars. It is regrettable that this kind of facility has not been duplicated in other parts of the world.

Professional journals are another way to develop a field of study. They provide mechanisms for professionals to share ideas, to learn about new books, and to discover trends. Until a year ago, there was no journal designed to build the social studies field internationally. The new *International Journal for Political Education,* edited by Willem Langeveld, a social studies educator at the University of Amsterdam, helps meet this need. Langeveld is assisted by a worldwide editorial board, including two Americans, and a number of "correspondents" whose job is to identify potential contributors.[10] All articles, regardless of the author's nationality, are published in English, thereby making the ideas accessible to American social studies teachers.

Several universities have encouraged contacts with professionals abroad, primarily by arranging educational tours for teachers to India, USSR, China, Nigeria, and other nations. The Social Studies Development Center at Indiana University has been engaged in an unusual cooperative effort with the Bundeszentrale für politische Bildung (Federal Center for Political Education) in the Federal Republic of Germany. In 1975, SSDC hosted a conference on political education in Germany and the United States, attended by approximately forty American and German specialists. The five-day conference was devoted to comparing ideas that influence "political education" (citizenship education) in the two nations and to examining some of the leading instructional programs used by their schools. In the fall of 1977, a follow-up conference that focused on the relationship between political socialization research and political education was held in Tutzing, Germany. Approximately sixty specialists from seven nations (the majority being German and American) attended this five-day meeting. Many of the conference papers have been published in both English and German in order to make them more generally available in both nations.

Further Efforts Needed to Internationalize Social Studies

While some steps have been taken to bring ideas and concerns in social studies from other countries to the attention of American social studies educators, many more are required. Following are a few suggestions that might be helpful.

Prepare Social Studies Specialists Who Are Fluent in Other Languages. It is unrealistic to expect that a majority of American social studies specialists will become fluent in languages other than English and thus begin to follow the social studies literature of other nations. It *is* both realistic and essential that the United States have *some* specialists who know a foreign language, who are informed about social studies developments in other countries, and who will interpret foreign literature for the rest of us. At one time, doctoral candidates were expected to be able to read at least one modern foreign language. Many universities have replaced this requirement with one or more "tool skills," such as statistics or computer science. It is important that the social studies field have some scholars able to enrich our profession with ideas borrowed from other societies.

International Conferences. Attention should be given to planning conferences that bring specialists from different parts of the world together to discuss mutual interests. Recent UNESCO conferences on social studies, moral education, and human rights have included social studies educators from the United States and other nations. While these have been useful, they have not been sufficient. Nor did the conferences sponsored by the Bundeszentrale für politische Bildung and the Social Studies Development Center described earlier do more than set a precedent. There should be at least one international conference every other year somewhere in the world that addresses important concerns of social studies educators.

New Publications. While Bulletins of this type can alert social studies educators to the need for international communication on professional issues, more and different publications are needed. *Social Education* should publish articles about social studies in other nations. Books about social studies in other nations should be written.[11] Reviews of books published abroad must find their way into American journals. Special publications aimed at cross-national comparisons must be undertaken. Until the volume of literature about social studies in other nations grows, social studies educators can hardly be faulted for the gaps in their knowledge.

Build an International Network on Behalf of Social Studies Educators. A number of nations have "national councils" for social studies, but there is no "international social studies council." It is probably premature to establish such an international council based upon individual memberships at the present time, but steps could be taken to link the various national councils so that they can become more familiar with each other's efforts. Members of national councils could then have opportunities to gain information about developments in other nations. National councils could agree to co-sponsor international meetings on topics of mutual interest and concern. They might lend support to journals such as the *International Journal of Political Education.* Such experiences would make it easier for universities sponsoring educational tours to other nations to arrange meetings between the participants and social studies authorities in the nations they are visiting.

Conclusion

American social studies educators have no monopoly on social studies ideas and practices. Granted, since 1945 the United States has played a leadership role in the development of this field, but increasingly leadership is being widely distributed in this arena as in many other aspects of social, economic, and political life. Americans have much to learn as well as to teach. As in any field, people must specialize. Most will find it difficult to keep abreast of social studies developments in other nations unless a few make this their professional priority. American social studies as a professional field will be stronger when the present imbalance is corrected.

NOTES

[1]In May, 1977, the National Council for the Social Studies had 883 members representing 60 nations other than the United States. Indeed, if the foreign members of NCSS were to organize as an affiliate or special interest group, they would outnumber any other existing organization within NCSS.

[2]In the meantime, the study of foreign languages in American schools declines steadily. According to the American Council on Education, we have become the only major nation in the world that does not teach a second language to most youth. Of 1977 high school graduates in the United States, fewer than 2% had *any* foreign language competence.

[3]Is it possible that social studies teachers abroad actually differ very little in these ways from a substantial number of American social studies teachers?

[4]Social studies has not been equally successful in former French African colonies, in part because the relationship between educated Africans in French colonies to French nationalists was of a different order than that of educated Africans in English colonies to English settlers. While seizing independence, former French colonies have tended to retain large amounts of French culture. Moreover, language presents no problem to Americans working in former English colonies, while there are few American social studies specialists capable of working easily in former French colonies even if French-speaking Africans were inclined to invite them.

[5]The History 13–16 Project was established at the University of Leeds in 1972. Its materials are now available commercially through Holmes McDougall, Allander House, 137–141 Leith Walk, Edinburgh EHN 86NS, Scotland.

[6]Those wishing a quick review of developments in England regarding research on history teaching might begin by reading *Teaching History,* No. 21 (June, 1978), published by the British Historical Association.

[7]For example, see *Moralogy Today: The Present Situation in Moralogy Studies and Their Tasks.* Chiba-Ken, Japan: Institute of Moralogy, 1974.

[8]NCSS Bulletin #51, *Defining the Social Studies*, was an effort at reaching a new, consensual definition of social studies after an exploration of its history and of the confusion surrounding its scope and purpose. NCSS Bulletin #52, *Building Rationales for Citizenship Education,* focused on the importance of strengthening the rationale and justification for citizenship education.

[9]For more details about the curriculum development aspects of the project, see *Political Education and Political Literacy,* ed. by Bernard Crick and Alex Porter. London: Longman Group Limited, 1978.

[10]*The International Journal of Political Education* is published quarterly by Elsevier Scientific Publishing Company, P.O. Box 211, Amsterdam, The Netherlands.

[11]A good example of such a book is *Social Studies in West German Schools: Firsthand Perspectives for Educators* by Wayne Dumas and William B. Lee. Columbia: University of Missouri Press, 1978.

Social Studies in the Federal Republic of Germany

Annette Kuhn

WHAT DOES SOCIAL STUDIES MEAN IN THE FEDERAL REPUBLIC OF GERMANY?

It is impossible to offer a single satisfactory definition of social studies within German schools. Despite the use of such expressions as "soziale Studien," there is no term that is equivalent to the American phrase "social studies." When discussing social studies in Germany, at least six different terms—"Sozialkunde," "Gemeinschaftskunde," "soziale Studien," "politische Bildung," "Gesellschaftslehre," and "Geschichte/Politik"—may be used.

The confusion over terminology reflects the confusion that besets other aspects of social studies. The different expressions that stand for social studies indicate the absence of agreement in the Federal Republic of Germany on the goals, content, structure, and theoretical basis for social studies.[1] They also serve as reminders of the various approaches taken by reformers to introduce social studies into the curriculum during the past three decades.

The social studies reform has taken place in two distinct periods in post-war Germany. The first period, from 1945 to approximately the mid-1960s when West Germany regained its sovereignty as a provisional, divided nation, featured efforts to introduce "political education" into the school curriculum by both the Federal government and by the states. These efforts appeared under different labels: "Sozialkunde," "Gemeinschaftskunde," "Staatsbürgerkunde," and "politische Bildung," which varied from one another in degree and substance. Nevertheless, they all reflected a common concern: to prepare young people who would possess the political knowledge, values, and skills appropriate to democratic government as practiced in the Federal Republic of Germany. The emphasis upon political education, or citizenship education, occurred before there was an interest in social studies broadly.

The second period of social studies reform, extending from the mid-1960s to the present, was prompted by a general interest in nationwide curriculum reform, by the education reform programs advocated by the Liberal and Social Democratic parties, and by a general tendency toward fundamental changes in educational policy and beliefs. These forces led to a reconsideration of the nature and purpose of political education. The "new political education" that emerged constitutes the core of social studies in the Federal Republic of Germany.

As a new conception of political education, social studies means something quite different from the type of political education that was introduced in schools during the first postwar decade. In the first period, political education was considered to be an additional school subject (like "civics" in the United States) or as a general educational principle ("Unterrichtsprinzip"), compatible with traditional school courses, especially history. But social studies goes beyond this type of political education in many ways. Social studies is based upon theoretical conceptions that are different from those underlying the traditional curricula of German schools; it calls for changes in existing courses; and it depends upon fundamental reforms in the traditional organization of schools. Thus, it is not possible to discuss social studies in West Germany without considering problems of social change or accepting the need to reorganize the system of public schools.

During the second period, competing conceptions of social studies flourished. The new terms "Gesellschaftslehre," "Politik," "soziale Studien," and "Geschichte/Politik" symbolize some of the alternative approaches. Perhaps all can be accommodated by thinking of social studies in Germany as a new conception of political education that is part of a general reform movement directed at changing the entire educational system.[2]

In order to comprehend the nature of social studies in Germany, it is important to understand the characteristics of German social and political life and the structure of the German school system following World War II. These two elements provide a frame of reference for examining social studies within the Federal Republic of Germany. This frame of reference also contains an assumption: neither the public school system as it is presently organized nor the social and political structures as restored after 1945 encourages the massive educational changes that must occur before social studies can be fully implemented. The section that follows will clarify how the structure of the German school system inhibits the development of social studies.

Post-War Organization of the German Public Schools

Efforts after 1945 to establish a modern German school system in harmony with the imperatives of an industrialized nation and the principles of a democratic society failed.[3] Post-war politicians and educational leaders tried to overcome the National Socialist era by returning to former German philosophical and educational traditions. The revival of the idealistic thinking of the German classic tradition and the restoration of the humanistic tradition seemed to be the best guarantee for post-war Germany to regain its former reputation as a participant in Western European culture.

Most of the major, current problems affecting the German school system stem from the decision to re-establish schools after World War II on the pre-democratic school traditions of the nineteenth century.[4] Although compulsory primary education was introduced in Germany in the nineteenth century, primary schools for the masses were clearly distinguished from the classical education long available to the upper classes and the intellectual elite. The new primary school was to provide the type of education deemed essential to the nation's need for skilled industrial workers. Schools for the upper classes, however, provided preparation for the university and ultimately for the professions and for leadership positions in government. The curricula, educational goals, and mission of these two types of schools were vastly different from each other.

The development of two completely isolated school systems is due mainly to the role played by the German middle class in the nineteenth and early twentieth centuries.[5] Contrary to the political attitudes of the middle classes in England, France, and other Western countries, the German middle class did not strive for political power, responsibility, or democratic change in society. Therefore, in Germany, the growth of the middle class did not go hand-in-hand with political demands and successful educational reform movements. Since the German middle class adjusted itself to the feudal structure of society and to authoritarian forms of government, there seemed to be little need to change the educational system.

The distinction between education for the masses and education for the elite was maintained not only by the apolitical attitudes exhibited by the German middle class; German philosophers and educators also devised theories to justify the two-track system. Indeed, the existence of such theories contributed to the revival of the traditional school system after World War II. Although in 1918 educational reformers had succeeded in passing legislation requiring that all children, regardless of social class, must attend primary schools together, the educational system as a whole continued to reflect the ideals of a pre-democratic society, lending support to the traditional system of social classes.

Diagram #1 (p. 18) reveals the main features of the German school system today. It indicates the various types of schools and the alternative paths to acquire school degrees. It also reflects the social system of postwar West Germany.

The German educational system has often been compared to a dinner fork ("Gabelungssystem"), because the school system, like a fork, has three prongs.[6] Following an initial four-year experience in elementary school ("Grundschule"), that is attended by all regardless of social class, students are sorted into three separate forms of schooling: "Hauptschule," "Realschule," and "Gymnasium." The majority attend the "Hauptschule"; its graduates fill most of the non-professional occupational roles in the society. They are farmers, laborers, industrial workers, retail clerks, etc. After nine years of total schooling, many continue in apprenticeship training that links on-the-job instruction with a few hours of instruction each week in an academic setting. Some "Hauptschule" graduates may continue their studies in technical colleges.

18

Diagram 1*
The School System in the Federal Republic of Germany

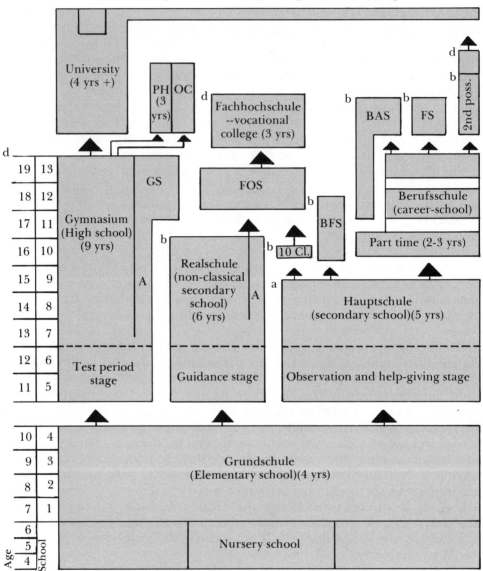

This diagram does not take into account special types of education and regulations applying in certain Federal states. The remarks made next to the fifth and sixth school year do not apply to the different kinds of school that may be attended by children aged eleven and twelve, but vary in differing permutations from one state to another.

Termination of education careers: a = Elementary education, b = "Secondary" education, c = Skilled vocational education, d = Advanced level education. Abbreviations: PH = Pädagogische Hochschule (teacher-training college), OC = other type of college, BAS = Berufsaufbauschule (advanced career training school), FS = Fachschule (technical school), GS = Grammar School, (H) BFS = (Hohere) Berufsfachschule (higher) specialist career training school, FOS = Fachoberschule (Specialist upper school), A = specialist high school.

Based upon a diagram that appears in Germany: Facts and Figures about the Two German States. Bonn: Federal Republic of Germany, Press and Information Office, 1973, p. 12.

The "Realschule" is designed to prepare people for upper-level, non-professional careers. Students may receive technical training. Some graduates find positions as middle-level bureaucrats. The assumption is that "Realschule" graduates do not require a classical education, but they must be more proficient in mathematics and language than those graduating from "Hauptschule." Thus, typical "Realschule" pupils study English as a foreign language while no foreign language is required in the "Hauptschule."

The "Gymnasium" is for those seeking entrance to the university. Until recently, one could attend a university only upon having completed an "Abitur," the degree conferred upon "Gymnasium" graduates; and all students with an "Abitur" were guaranteed a place in a university. As a result of some recent reforms, the number of "Gymnasium" graduates has grown so large that spaces in universities are no longer assured. This has added to the tension in German education.

While limited opportunities exist for students to transfer from one track to another—or even on rare occasions for a "Hauptschule" graduate to find a place in a university—the fact remains that the German educational system is highly differentiated, very selective, and based upon the principle of preserving and justifying the existing social and political system. Unlike the United States where education is intended, in theory at least if not always in practice, to encourage social mobility, the German school system intends to keep people in their own situations from one generation to another. German workers, graduates of "Hauptschule," see their children attend "Hauptschule" and assume the careers of their fathers and mothers. Wealthy, university-educated Germans send their children to the "Gymnasium." While success in schools and selection of tracks is supposedly based upon performance on tests and in class, in fact wealthy children have advantages over poor children. Their parents can hire tutors and provide enriched home opportunities, and the stigma for failure to succeed in school is greater for children of upper classes in Germany than is true in the United States. Moreover, career choices are made early, at the end of grade four. If at age ten a child misses by chance, birth, or poor grades the opportunity to qualify for the "Realschule" or the "Gymnasium," his or her opportunities in life are already sharply limited.

At the beginning of the 1960s, politicians became aware that the selective school system endangered economic progress. The Organization for Economic Cooperation and Development predicted that Western Germany would rank lowest among nine European countries regarding the numbers of high school graduates by 1970 (chart No. 1, p. 20).

Prominent scholars, such as Georg Picht, claimed that the German educational system would drive the nation into new catastrophes, if it did not adapt to the necessities of a modern industrial state and to the demands of a democratic society.[7] It was demonstrated that the German school system not only preserved an immobile and elitist social structure, but that it also contradicted fundamental rights guaranteed by the German constitution; namely the right of each citizen to acquire an education and the right to an equal opportunity to gain an adequate position in society (chart No. 2, p. 20).

20

Chart No. 2

OECD Survey on High School Graduates

			No. in thousands	% of growth
Jugoslawien (Yugoslavia)	1959 1970		38,1 94,4	148%
Norwegen (Norway)	1959 1970		4,9 13,0	165%
Frankreich (France)	1959 1970		59,1 150,0	154%
Belgien (Belgium)	1959 1970		10,4 20,8	100%
Schweden (Sweden)	1959 1970		10,5 25,0	138%
Italien (Italy)	1959 1970		55,6 116,6	110%
Danemark (Denmark)	1959 1970		3,8 8,5	124%
Niederlande (Netherlands)	1959 1970		10,0 20,0	100%
Bundesrep. Deutschland (Germany)	1959 1970		51,4 53,3	4%

Georg Picht, *Die deutsche Bildungskatastrophe (The German Educational Catastrophe)*, Olten/Freiburg: Walter Verlag, 1964, p. 27.

Chart No. 3

The Social Background of German University Students

		% of population Anteil an der Bevölkerung	% of students Anteil an den Studenten
Workers	Arbeiter	49,8	5,2
Employee	Angestellte	22,7	29,3
Businesspersons	Handel- und Ge- werbetreibende	10,6	14,5
Farmers	selbstandige Landwirte	8,7	3,5
State officials	Beamte	6,7	33,7
Free occupations	freie Berufe	1,5	12,4

Helmut Becker, H.D. Haller, H. Stubenrauch, G. Wilkending, *Das Curriculum, Praxis, Wissenschaft und Politik (Curriculum, Practice, Science, and Politics)*. München: Juventa-Verlag, 1974, p. 172.

These reports coincided with the first economic crisis in post-war Germany, with a change in government and with signs of social unrest and deep dissatisfaction among the German people, especially among the youth. All of these events are part of the social and political background of the nationwide educational reform movement that started in the middle of the 1960s for the purpose of reorganizing the traditional German school system. Both the three-track system ("Hauptschule," "Realschule," and "Gymnasium") and the distinctions that separated academic training from occupational education were to be replaced by a system of modern, cooperative or comprehensive schools ("kooperative Schule," "Gesamtschule," "Gesamthochschule") that would bring both academic and non-academic studies together at one site and that would serve all social classes. The analogue would be the comprehensive high schools in the United States. Needless to say, this ambitious reform program implied a fundamentally new outlook for political education.[8]

Political Education in Post-War Germany

The first fifteen years of post-war German political education was characterized by many different approaches, stressing either national values, pre-political social behavior, or political behavior in compliance with the existing democratic institutions of the German Federal Republic. Despite differences among the main approaches, all had much in common. All sought to convey attitudes beneficial to society by urging acceptance of German democracy as a form of government. Western Germany, as it was established by the Western allied forces after the war, was taken for granted as an inevitable institution, guaranteeing to Germans freedom and economic and social development.[9] Many observers of post-war Germany, such as Golo Mann, were confident that the new republic was moving toward democracy and a classless society. For post-war political education, democracy was not a debatable issue. Democracy was seen as merely a political framework, a welcome alternative to National Socialism or communism, which were both unacceptable.

Under these conditions, no new conception of political education was developed. Instead of considering the post-war social and political situation in West Germany as a unique moral and political challenge, older political education traditions were revived and foreign ones imported. This is true of the revival of the humanism and idealistic Hegelian thought on the moral values of the state, represented by such philosophers as Theodore Litt and Eduard Spranger, of the reintroduction of education about governmental institutions ("Institutionskunde") as it was practiced in the Weimar Republic, and of the adoption of John Dewey's ideas as a theoretical basis for social education ("Partnerschaftserziehung").

Political Education Gains Special Attention. Two political issues helped arouse interest in political education around 1955: the desecration of synagogues and Jewish cemeteries and the confrontation with communism. Both of these issues led to new state resolutions, emphasizing the importance of the specific political elements of political education. The term "politische Erziehung," officially introduced in 1955, implied that political education should go beyond the existing pre-political concepts of social education ("Sozialkunde," "Gemeinschaftskunde"). Very soon, political education was introduced into all types of schools. It was made obligatory in the "Hauptschule." Academies for political education, established initially for adult education, were asked to support these efforts. As a result of governmental decrees of 1960 ("Ostkundeerlass," "Totalitarismuserlass"), new guidelines for history and political education were developed that stressed the importance of the treatment of both National Socialism and communism as totalitarian regimes.

In retrospect, this first period of political education may be judged faulty in several respects. Empirical studies on the effects of political education show that, although the interest of students in political education had grown constantly within these years of increased schooling, German students were not prepared to analyze social and political issues and to make their own value judgments. The humanistic tradition, dominant in history and German teaching, apparently neutralized the impact of political thought, and instruction about democratic institutions had failed to encourage participatory attitudes on the part of youth. Anti-totalitarianism, treating both National Socialism and communism as two different expressions of the same phenomena, proved inadequate. In the mid-1960s, this phase of political education entered into a crisis.

New Conceptions of Social Studies in Germany. As mentioned earlier, the mid-1960s was a period of educational ferment in the Federal Republic of Germany. New conceptions of social studies appeared as a response to the political, social, and economic crisis Germany faced during this period. New social studies guidelines prepared by some of the states reflect the radical change in political attitudes among many Germans during this time.

It would be a mistake, however, to view this development as solely a German phenomenon. Political and social unrest and student revolts were common to nearly all of the industrialized Western democracies. Therefore, demands for changes in Germany shared some common features with demands raised in other nations. Yet, certain reactions to the political and social crisis of the mid-1960s were peculiar to Germany and indicative of special German approaches toward a new conception of social studies.

Earlier, social studies was described as a new conception of political education that is part of a general reform movement directed at changing the entire educational system. Three factors seemed especially influential in affecting the development of social studies in Germany. These were the politicization of reform proposals; the influence of American empirical-based, curriculum development theories; and the impact of "Kritische Theorie" (Critical Theory) as a philosophical system.

The announcement that school decisions often become objects of political controversy provides no surprise for American educators. Issues of busing, of assignment of pupils, and even of selection of textbooks often arouse bitter debate among citizens in an American community. But rarely does school politics become partisan politics in the United States.

Early age is no deterrent to the development of skills in schools in the Federal Republic of Germany. Used with permission of the European Community Information Service, Washington, D.C.

The Republican party does not favor one kind of school or curriculum while the Democrats prefer another. But in the Federal Republic of Germany, educational proposals assume greater importance in political party platforms than assertions about foreign policy or farm policy. In the past, the Christian Democrats have favored traditional patterns of school organization; they have supported the *status quo*. The Social Democrats, in contrast, have advocated major school reforms, have urged the establishment of comprehensive schools ("Gesamtschule"), and have promoted changes in the school curriculum. For example, in the state of Hesse, which has been controlled by the Social Democrats, educators prepared new guidelines for social studies ("Gesellschaftslehre") that integrated history, geography, and political education into a single course. Their intention was to narrow the gap between stated objectives regarding democratic citizenship, the content of courses, and the organization of schools. Thus, the guidelines also depended upon reforming the structure of schools by replacing traditional schools with comprehensive schools. In Hesse, and in each of the other states, proposals for major changes in the curriculum and the organization of schools are fought out by the parties during election campaigns. Thus, successful reform ultimately involves convincing the electorate of the desirability of change.[10]

Social studies was also affected by new curriculum theories, especially those imported from the United States. Instead of relying on the idealistic tradition of German philosophy as an adequate basis for deriving general learning objectives for political education, German curriculum reformers began to employ new criteria for selecting objectives, for preparing school materials, and for developing guidelines. They sought to be more scientific in their effort to measure instructional effects and to study learning processes. Saul Robinsohn's book *Bildungsreform als Revision des Curriculum (Educational Reform through Curriculum Revision)* influenced many. New social studies guidelines such as "Richtlinien Gesellschaftslehre" in Hesse and "Richtlinien Politik" in Northrhine-Westphalia drew upon the new curriculum theories and approaches.

But German efforts were not merely copies of American work.[11] New ideas were introduced that enabled German educators to break new paths for others to follow. Above all, the basic principles of "critical theory" ("Kritische Theorie") became the dominant school of social and political thought during the late 1960s and early 1970s. Critical theory, associated with a group of scholars in Frankfurt, most notably Jürgen Habermas, influenced the German adaptation of American curriculum theory and strategy and contributed to a new and critical conception of the social studies. Very few American social studies specialists are familiar with the ideas that comprise "critical theory," except to the degree that they know the writings of Herbert Marcuse, who was closely linked to the Frankfurt group. In Germany, however, the impact has been great, although the ideas are controversial and have deeply divided social studies educators. The curricular impact of "critical theory" may be seen best in the Hesse "Rahmenrichtlinien Gesellschaftslehre."[12]

These three elements—the politicization of educational reform, the influence of American curriculum development theories, and "Kritische Theorie"—have been significant in the development of a "new social studies in Germany." However, the full achievement of a true social studies in German schools will not take place without changes leading to a greater democratization of the society and the restructuring of schools.[13]

WHAT IS THE RELATIONSHIP BETWEEN SOCIAL STUDIES AND CITIZENSHIP EDUCATION?

Unlike social studies, citizenship education was not introduced explicitly in the German post-war educational system, either in the field of history or in social studies. This may seem surprising, because citizenship education is a main objective both in history and in political education. Students are expected to develop a consciousness of German citizenship in accordance with the basic values ("Grundwerte") of the constitution of the Federal Republic of Germany. In this broad, vague sense, citizenship education has been generally accepted as part of political education.

Despite this acknowledgment of citizenship as a value objective, citizenship education has not been developed explicitly. The term itself ("Staatsbürgerkunde") has not been used either in curriculum guidelines or in theories of political education.

Historical Development of Citizenship Education in Germany

In the nineteenth century, citizenship education was undoubtedly the guiding objective for history teaching. It was also the hidden curriculum in school teaching. Citizenship education meant imposing upon all German students, regardless of their heritage and their social status, feelings of absolute, uncritical allegiance to the ideals of the Prussian monarchy. Unfortunately, as a military and bureaucratic system, the basic values of Prussian Germany were absolutely contrary to the development of liberal and democratic attitudes in German society.

Traditionally, the ideological framework for citizenship education in Germany has been the idealistic—in later German history perverted—notion of the state as a legal and moral entity. This idealistic notion was detached from concrete social life, devoid of any acknowledgment of social struggle, and unembarrassed by the social reality of the "Kaiserreich." Needless to say, citizenship education tended to make pupils blind, law-abiding citizens, insensitive to the values of social justice and of a democratic society. Although liberal reformers tried to discard this tradition and give support to a new kind of citizenship education during the Weimar Republic (1918–1933), it continued to be substantially what it was during the monarchy. As a result of its commitment to a theory of the state, it was completely unable to resist National Socialism. Residues of this theory pose a danger to German political education even at the present time.

This idealistic tradition of citizenship education was opposed by the majority of historians and history teachers after 1949. Aware of the consequences of traditional citizenship education beliefs, they tried to escape the problem by avoiding the instrumental use of history to promote citizenship education and by reverting to historicism and accepting the predemocratic traditions of history as a cultural entity in the sense of Leopold von Ranke. Needless to say, this attitude did not help to solve the problems of citizenship education.

The tendency towards apolitical history teaching has been discarded during the 1960s. Characteristic of the new developments are the speeches on the goals of public history teaching by President Heinemann, who pointed out the importance of reinterpreting the German past and reconsidering German democratic and socialist traditions.

Today, historians and history teachers are being challenged by new demands for citizenship education through history, but a citizenship education unlike older forms of citizenship education and its underlying ideology. The new form of citizenship education in history is based on a critical view of social reality and of the value objectives compatible with a democratic society. It hopes to develop an attitude of critical identification with German traditions, especially the neglected democratic and socialist traditions of the German past.

Political Problems of Citizenship Education

Citizenship education is not a clearly defined subject matter or objective in social studies. In part this stems from the fact that Germany is not a unified nation. Since West Germany has no clearly defined national identity, it is difficult to link citizenship education goals with Germany's present national status.

During the 1950s, conservatives interpreted social studies as a type of citizenship education, based mainly on traditional values and state loyalty. In doing so, they regarded the Federal Republic of Germany as the only legitimate heir of German culture and denied the existence of the German Democratic Republic as an independent, legal state. This conservative view of social studies, dominant during the Adenauer era, has lost much of its influence under the present coalition government of Liberals and Social Democrats. At the same time, the new conceptions of social studies, which have been encouraged during the last ten years, have given little attention to citizenship education. This shortcoming is now being recognized.

Citizenship education in Germany faces yet another difficulty. Not only do Germans lack a unified national state, based upon a set of political values embraced by all Germans, they also lack a solid, democratic tradition. Germany's historical background has prompted at least two different approaches towards citizenship education. Both approaches are compatible with our democratic system, although they disagree on nearly all substantial questions about citizenship education. One is a conservative approach, stressing the values of authority, state power and state law, order and discipline, and advocating a national citizenship education. The other is a liberal and social-democratic approach, based on the principle of social development, accepting social conflicts as a legitimate expression of social change, and aiming at educational goals such as critical, democratic citizenship.

Theoretical Implications of Citizenship Education

Citizenship education requires a minimum of consensus on fundamental political values. This consensus does not exist in Germany. As noted earlier, Germany must struggle with the twofold dilemma of a weak democratic tradition and a divided nation. These two elements present a particular challenge to conservative positions which must compete with other political educational theories without at the same time falling into reactionary or nationalistic positions. The liberal and social-democratic approaches to citizenship education vary from each other only in degree, not in fundamentals. The social-democratic view has partly adopted basic ideas of the "Kritische Theorie" of the Frankfurt School of Philosophy.

The existence of competing approaches need not be viewed as a weakness in a pluralistic society. They create the conditions for new educational choices; they blunt the possibility of one set of values becoming dominant over others. Liberal and social-democratic advocates accept the conflict between different sets of values as an essential part of citizenship education ("Konfliktdidaktik").

WHAT ARE THE MAJOR ISSUES IN THE SOCIAL STUDIES IN THE FEDERAL REPUBLIC OF GERMANY?

In one sense the major issues facing social studies in Germany have been discussed. What social studies will or can become is dependent upon the direction of social change in Germany and the results of institutional school reform. Previous research on instruction in the comprehensive schools ("Gesamtschule") confirms the hypothesis that the new type of school is far more congenial to the learning objectives called for in the new social studies than the traditional system with its three tracks.[14] Nevertheless, resistance to changing over to the new form of schooling is strong, and one cannot predict whether the school reform movement will be ultimately successful or not. If it fails, the future for social studies is bleak.

Citizenship education is also likely to be an important issue for reasons stated earlier. Nationalistic, anti-socialist, and anti-democratic aspects of the traditional kind of citizenship education have had enduring effects on the perspectives and behavior of the German people. This tradition, still very much alive, has made educational reformers reluctant to pursue citizenship education goals. Nevertheless, the need for a modern, enlightened, emancipatory kind of citizenship education is needed. Social studies educators know that values such as national allegiance, overemphasized and perverted in the past, cannot be ignored. They can be introduced again in the curriculum provided it is done in a critical manner, guaranteeing democratic, non-nationalistic value judgments.

Clearly, one issue that will continue to draw attention is the role history should play in the curriculum. Some reformers seek to integrate history and social studies and form new courses.[15] Others try to affect the kind of history that is taught while preserving the role of history as a separate subject in schools. Efforts to apply critical theory to the study of history will continue to arouse debate.

Finally, moral education has attracted considerable interest recently.[16] Jürgen Habermas has introduced Lawrence Kohlberg's ideas to German educators, and efforts are underway to link ideas relating to the moral development of children to theories of society and history.[17] Behind this effort is a concern to develop curricula that have relevance beyond the boundaries of a single nation, that might contribute to a "one-world" conception of citizenship education.

Thus, the future of social studies in Germany is unclear. It is a time of considerable ferment. What finally emerges will likely represent a compromise among the traditions of the past, ideas imported from the United States, and the forces of social change operating in Germany today.

NOTES

[1] Wolfgang Hilligen, *Zur Didaktik der politischen Unterrichts I (Toward a Didactic of Political Instruction)*. Opladen: Leske, 1975. Hilligen gives an overall view of the different concepts.

[2] Rolf Schmiederer, *Zwischen Affirmation und Reformismus, Politische Bildung in Westdeutschland seit 1945 (Between Affirmation and Reform: Political Education in West Germany Since 1945)*. Frankfurt: Europäische Verlagsanstalt, 1972. This book is introductory to the history of political education in Western Germany.

[3] Eberhard Schmidt, *Die verhinderte Neuordnung 1945–1952 (The Thwarted Reorganization)*. Frankfurt: 1970.

[4] Ilse/Klafki, Dahmer, Wolfgang (Hg.), *Geschichtswissenschaftliche Pädagogik am Ausgang ihrer Epoche (The Pedagogy of the Science of History at the End of Its Epoch)*. Weinheim: Beltz, 1968.

[5] Detlef K. Müller, *Sozialstruktur und Schulsystem: Aspekte zum Strukturwandel des Schulwesens im 19. Jahrhundert (Social Structure and the School System: Aspects toward Structural Change of the Schools in the Nineteenth Century)*. Göttingen: Vandenhoeck & Ruprecht, 1977.

[6] Frank Achtenhagen, "Berufsausbildung," in: *Handbuch pädagogischer Grundbegriffe*, Bd. 1, hg. von J. Speck und G. Wehle ("Vocational Training" in *Handbook of Pedagogical Basic Terms*, Vol. 1). München: Kösel-Verlag, 1970 S. 82–112.

[7] Georg Picht, *Die deutsche Bildungskatastrophe, Analyse und Dokumentation (The German Educational Catastrophe, Analysis and Documentation)*. Olten/Freiburg i.B.: Walter Verlag, 1964.

[8] Jürgen Habermas, *Legitimationsprobleme im Spätkapitalismus (The Problem of Legitimization in Late Capitalism)*. Frankfurt: Suhrkamp, 1973.

[9] Alfred Grosser, *Die Bonner Demokratie (The Bonn Democracy)*. Düsseldorf: Droste, 1960.

[10] F. Naschold, *Organisation und Demokratie (Organization and Democracy)*. Stuttgart: Kohlhammer, 1969.

[11] D. Elbers, *Curriculumreformen in den USA: Ein Bericht über theoretische Ansätze und praktische Reformverfahren. Studien und Berichte 28. (Curriculum Reform in the USA: A Report on Theoretical Approaches and Practical Reform Procedures. Studies and Reports)*. Berlin: Max-Planck-Institut für Bildungsforschung, 1973.

[12] The discussion on the "politics guidelines" in Nordrhein-Westfalen is typical for a critical approach to the adaptation of curriculum theory. Rolf Schörken (Hg.), *Curriculum 'Politik': Von der Curriculumtheorie zur Unterrichtspraxis (The "Politics" Curriculum: From a Theory of Curriculum to the Practice of Instruction)*. Opladen: Leske, 1974.

[13] Hans-G. Rolff, *Sozialisation und Auslese durch die Schule (Socialization and Selection Through the Schools)*. Heidelberg: 1972.

[14] Helmut Fend u.a., *Sozialisationseffekte der Schule (The Socialization Effects of Schools)*. Weinheim: Beltz, 1976.

[15] One example for this approach can be found in: Rolf Schörken, "Kriterien für einen lernzielorientierten Geschichtsunterricht," in: *Die Funktion der Geschichte in unserer Zeit* ("Criteria for Goal-Oriented History Instruction" in *The Function of History in Our Time*). Stuttgart: Klett, 1975, S. 280–293.

[16] Jürgen Habermas, "Können komplexe Gesellschaften eine vernünftige Identität ausbilden?" in: *Zur Rekonstruktion des Historischen Materialismus* ("Can Complex Societies Build a Meaningful Identity?" in *Toward a Reconstruction of Historical Materialism*). Frankfurt: Suhrkamp, 1976, S. 92–128.

[17] The leading theoretical book is by Jürgen Habermas, *Zur Rekonstruktion des Historischen Materialismus (Toward a Reconstruction of Historical Materialism)*. Frankfurt: Suhrkamp, 1976.

Social Studies in Thailand

Absorn Meesing

WHAT DOES SOCIAL STUDIES MEAN IN THAILAND?

The concept of social studies is a fairly recent one in Thailand, but the practice of social studies has a rich tradition. Before the government established the modern Thai educational system, Buddhist monasteries provided instruction for boys. These young men chanted Buddhist prayers and learned reading, writing, and arithmetic. While the Buddhist monks were not called social studies teachers, nevertheless they introduced boys to the values and practices of Thai society.

Social studies instruction occurred in still other ways for those able to attend Buddhist schools and those who did not. If social studies is intended to help youth become good members of the society, the responsibility for such socialization was shared effectively by parents and other adults. From them Thai children acquired a knowledge of Thai customs, ethics, and proper social behavior.

Traditional education in Thailand was affected by colonial expansion, especially that of France and Great Britain, during the period 1867–1893. Although the Thai people were able to maintain their independence, in part a consequence of the accommodating diplomacy of their leaders,[1] Western ideas penetrated various aspects of Thai society. For example, largely as a result of British influence, geography and history were introduced as regular school courses in 1895. Later civics and ethics were added.[2] Until very recently, these four disciplines represented Thailand's approach to social studies. The traditional approach involving socialization into the mores, customs, and beliefs gradually gave way to a more academic orientation, especially through courses in history and geography.

Until 1932, when a political revolution transformed an absolute monarchy into a constitutional monarchy, the Thai educational system as a whole, as well as its component subjects, reflected an amalgamation of traditional and Western (especially English) influences. With the advent of a constitutional monarchy, education was identified as one of the six major tasks for the new regime; and social studies was assigned new im-

Part of a typical Thai classroom, not necessarily social studies. It is an eighth-grade class with 40 students.

portance because of the need to prepare the Thai people for new and unfamiliar roles in a democratic society. Civics and ethics were expanded. New topics—such as constitutional government, elections, taxation, government ministries and their functions—were added to the curriculum.

One aspect that did not change as a result of the revolution was the administration of education. Both prior to and after the revolution, Thailand's education was centrally administered. Centralization has served not only to ensure more effective supervision and control and to maintain national standards; it also contributed to national unity, promoting public attitudes aimed at strengthening the kingdom and resisting colonialism.[3] The effect for social studies was to guarantee that all students received identical amounts of social studies instruction whatever emphasis was in vogue.

The close of World War II led to new influences in Thai education. Some Thais who had lived abroad throughout the war returned. Some students were sent overseas for study. Together these two groups contributed new kinds of professional training in education. New conditions in Thailand coupled with Thai scholars with Western training and experience made change inevitable. Within social studies this period marked a decline in the status of geography and ancient history and new attention to contemporary history and the history of Eastern nations. Increasingly, the content of each discipline acquired a Western flavor. Despite these trends, educators debated the relevance of a study of other civilizations for Thai society.[4]

The curriculum reform of 1960 was influenced mightily by Americans. Emphasis shifted from a concentration on the basic skills of reading, writing, and computation to subjects that contributed more to children's social and moral development.[5] The government accepted a responsibility to provide education for all in accordance with their abilities. The overall purposes of education were to produce good citizens who were healthy, responsible, well-disciplined, democratic-minded, cultured, and moral individuals. Education was organized so as to satisfy the needs of individuals while promoting national, economic development and governmental policies.

The term "social studies" was not used in Thailand until the 1960 reform. Even then, the term was used merely to group the four major disciplines of history, geography, civics, and ethics.[6] The courses continued to be listed separately in the curriculum and the instructional procedures used by each changed only slightly. The main changes occurred in the elementary grades where somewhat greater attention was given to social learning and somewhat less emphasis was placed upon academic knowledge. Therefore, despite progressive new goals and objectives, the actual content and instructional procedures employed drew heavily upon the past.

The curriculum reform of 1960 has with minor alterations remained in force until the present. A new curriculum reform, launched in 1978, will become fully operative over the next six years. Since the 1960 reform has been so significant and will continue to be important for several more years, it is important to describe it in some detail so that the reader will have a better grasp of social studies in Thailand.

Social Studies Under the 1960 Curriculum Reform[7]

By law all children are expected to complete an elementary school education (grades one through seven). In fact, it has not been possible to enforce this law in every region of the nation. Therefore, some children receive only four years of schooling.

Elementary School Social Studies. Social studies begins in grade one, which children enter at six years of age. Topics of study include "Home and Family Relations," "School Life," "Life in the Community," "Festivals and Holidays," and "News and Happenings." By grade four, the amount of time devoted to social studies has doubled. At this level children study physical geography of the world, geography of Thailand and neighboring nations, map reading and drawing, Thai history, lives of great persons, Thai government, the rights and duties of Thai citizens, morality and Thai culture, family and community responsibilities, and current events. By the time a student completes fourth grade, he or she will have spent 840 periods studying social studies.

As a group, elementary school teachers are poorly prepared to teach social studies. Research on the lower primary schools from 1963–1965 revealed that 65% of grade one social studies teachers found the social studies objectives provided by the curriculum guide to be unclear; 62% did not fully understand the content they were to teach; and 60% found the teaching instructions confusing.[8] As a result, teachers tend to depend almost entirely upon the textbook for guidance.

Social studies teachers are largely free to employ any teaching methods they wish. Dr. Aree Sankachawee once noted that during the last 100 years, good Thai teachers have used methods that are compatible with those recommended by modern educational philosophy and psychology.[9] Unfortunately, the techniques used by these gifted teachers have not been given sufficient dissemination.[10] In most classrooms the majority of time is spent by either the teacher talking (lecturing or asking questions) or the students' working quietly on exercises. Students are expected to listen, take notes, read the textbook, and answer questions.[11] Students are given very little practical experience that would promote and add zest to discussion and aid understanding.

Lower Secondary School Social Studies. Secondary schools are divided into two levels: lower secondary schools and upper secondary schools. There are also two curriculum "tracks": vocational and general. The most academically talented, especially those wishing to attend a university or college, follow the general program of studies. Less academically able students enroll in the vocational program. All students, regardless of career ambitions, spend three years in the lower secondary school, grades eight–ten. Vocational students devote three years to upper secondary education while general students complete their studies in two years. Because vocational studies lack the prestige of general studies, a higher proportion of students follow the latter track rather than the former.[12]

In the lower secondary school, general students have four social studies classes each week. All of the courses are required. Vocational students have only two periods of social studies each week. Both tracks require one period each of civics and ethics, which are usually taught separately. Civics focuses especially on social behavior, duties of citizens, operation of government, and national security. Because the last topic does not cover material learned previously in the elementary grades, it is the most popular.

Buddhism lies at the core of all ethics teaching. It is understandable why the content of ethics courses has been least affected by various revisions of the curriculum. The same topics are treated in one grade after another but at somewhat greater depth as the children advance from one grade level to another. Following are the topics typically treated in grade ten ethics classes:

- the life-stories of Buddha's disciples
- Buddhist obligations
- mindfulness and recollection—the two qualities that preserve all virtues
- the three basic evils—greed, malice, and illusion
- the four qualities that lead to success—interest, perseverance, study, and critical evaluation
- the virtues of a householder
- the four qualities that win friendship—generosity, gentle speech, helpfulness, and consistent behavior
- Buddhist proverbs

General students study geography and history three times each week while vocational students have such classes only once each week. Both

Buddhist monks are often asked to participate in planning and teaching classes in ethics.

groups of students study the economic geography of Thailand and other leading nations in Asia, Europe, North America, and Australia. In addition, general students study the regional and physical geography of these nations. Map reading and drawing are emphasized throughout. Compared to American students, Thai students devote much greater attention to geography and much less attention to history and the other social sciences.

In general, geography and history classes are more interesting to the majority of students than are the classes in civics and ethics. There is greater competition for grades by students; history and geography teachers tend to be better qualified than civics and ethics teachers.[13]

Geography classes tend to stress student learning of facts and principles rather than the analysis of the effects of environment on human life or the relationship of human beings and their environment. History stresses memorization of important events and the activities of particular kings. Undue emphasis is given to political history and too little to cultural history. This leads to parrot-like learning rather than any true understanding or appreciation of the former Thai kings' rule.

Teaching methods are similar to those used in elementary schools. Teacher-lecture is the principal technique. Some teachers encourage students' participation in class discussion, but students have become so used to being passive that such attempts are often ineffective. Individual and group investigations are inhibited by poor library resources.[14] Outside-of-classroom activities are not favored because they are viewed as taking much time for very little genuine learning. Teachers are judged primarily by how well their students perform on final examinations.[15]

Geography teachers often have more visual aids to assist their instruction than do teachers of other social studies courses.

Upper Secondary School Social Studies. The social studies a student receives in upper secondary schools depends upon whether the person is a general or a vocational student, and—if in the general program—what career he or she has selected. Those in the general track may select among three options: (1) The Science program is usually selected by the best students in science and mathematics. Graduates of this program pursue further university studies in engineering, medicine, etc. This program has the highest status. (2) The Arts program is for students interested in English and the humanities. Graduates continue their studies in departments of humanities, social science, language arts, etc., when they enter college. (3) The third program is a very general one for the least able students in the general program. It is assumed that these students will have difficulty passing university entrance examinations.

All students—whether in the general or vocational program—take a common core of social studies subjects. While the core social studies program required of all students continues the study of civics and ethics begun in the elementary grades, social science disciplines such as sociology and economics are also included. Students examine Thai social structure, social trends, and Thailand's social and economic development. Geography and history in the upper secondary schools tend to focus on foreign nations more so than in the lower grades. The core subjects are offered three periods each week. Each course extends over a two-year period. This means that when reviewing for the Ministry of Education final examination, a student must review two years' work for each course.

Beyond this core, the students in the Arts track of the general program are required to enroll in additional courses that form a quite different approach to social studies. General students who are in the track for less able students may also take up to two courses as electives. Neither students in the Science track of the general program nor vocational students have opportunities to take the most interesting, topical social studies courses. The alternative program in social studies is somewhat more appealing than the core program. In 1975, thirteen elective courses were established that include such course titles as "Population Education," "Social Problems of Thai Society," "International Problems," "Mapping," "World Religions," "The World at Present and Future." It is unfortunate that these courses are not required of all. Students taking these courses also meet three periods per week.

Recent Reform in the Social Studies Curriculum

On October 6, 1976, an important event occurred at Thamasat University; this event was to have important implications for social studies in Thailand. On that day, some University students hung the Crown Prince in effigy and burned many books. To some observers the three supreme institutions—the nation, Buddhism, and the king—were under assault.

The student rebellion on October 6 came at the end of six years of political instability that had witnessed six changes in government, including three coups. Moreover, economic problems had worsened. Throughout this period, there had also been mounting criticism of the educational system, leading to the appointment of various governmental committees to draft recommended changes.

It is important to note that while the student uprising on October 6, 1976 gave a certain urgency to the reform of education and influenced its ideology, the weaknesses of the existing system had been identified before 1976; and the reforms that were later approved were based largely on the work of key national committees that had reported their efforts prior to 1976. For example, a 1974 report had offered these observations on the teaching of social studies in the primary grades:[16]

1. Social studies topics depend heavily upon geography, history, civics, and ethics. The achievement of basic social studies objectives requires the use of other social sciences as well.
2. The content of each social studies course is poorly organized. Poor articulation among the four social studies courses fosters confusion and misunderstanding.
3. The content of the courses matches poorly with the stated objectives. Undue reliance is given to the transmission of academic-oriented factual knowledge. Too little attention is devoted to helping students grasp social processes and social science methods and concepts.
4. The existing program fails to encourage critical thinking.

In the same year, a report on secondary school social studies appeared. This report recommended that the study of the Thai language and social studies constitute the only required courses at the upper secondary grades because these courses fostered social unity. Other courses—e.g., mathematics, science, English, physical education—could be required at

Thai youth are encouraged to assume responsibility for the care and maintenance of their school. In this picture, students are working together on "Campus Development Day."

the lower secondary grades but should become electives in the upper grades. The committee further recommended that the amount of time devoted to geography and history be reduced in order to save time for more interesting topics and that the effort to insert full courses in other social sciences be resisted. Finally, the committee argued that the system of offering one-year-long courses in the lower secondary schools and two-year-long courses at the upper secondary grades be discontinued. Such courses should be replaced by semester-long courses.[17]

In 1977, the cabinet announced a new National Scheme of Education.[18] Among its important features were:

1. A change in the organization of schools from a 7-3-2 pattern to a 6-3-3 system.
2. A proclamation that the purpose of education was to prepare citizens who could think for themselves, act intelligently, solve problems, and participate in society. Such citizens should become lawful, patriotic members of society who believe firmly in their religion and in democratic government with the king as Head of State.
3. The decentralization of schooling with local authorities given greater responsibility over the planning, development, and evaluation of the curriculum.[19]
4. Admission that education can take various forms while responding to the needs of Thai society.

During the same year, a new curriculum plan was unveiled. This plan, labelled "Curriculum 78," became officially in force in May, 1978, although further time will pass before all of its aspects will become fully operational in all schools

Primary School Reforms. Primary education is compulsory for all youth from grades 1–6. The basic principle of primary education is to develop national unity. A main goal is to help children become useful members of their communities and society as a whole.

The "experiences" or content of the primary school curriculum are organized into four major groups: basic skills (Thai language and mathematics), life experience (personal and social problem-solving processes), character education (activities for developing habits of ethical character), and work experience. Social studies is part of the "life experience" segment of the curriculum which comprises 20 percent of the total school time in grades one and two and 25 percent of the time in grades three through six. As a result of its integration into "life experience," social studies as a separate field no longer exists in the primary grades.

"Life experience" is organized into twelve units. These are: "Living Things," "Life at Home," "Our Community," "The Thai Nation," "News and Holidays," "Making a Living," "Energy and Substance," "Universe and Space," "Neighboring Countries," "Communication," "Population Education," and "Politics and Government." It should be obvious that while social studies has disappeared as a separate field, many traditional topics remain in the curriculum. It is also evident that "life experiences" also seeks to integrate science and health into its content.

What American teachers would describe as moral education or values education appears in that portion of the curriculum labeled "character education." The emphasis in "character education" is less upon learning a specific body of knowledge and more upon cultivating certain habits of behavior. Thirty valuable virtues are emphasized throughout the six primary grades. There will be no written exams. Student achievement will be judged primarily by teachers' observations of student behavior.

No textbooks are being developed for either the "life experience" or "character education" segments of the curriculum. Teachers will be provided with detailed teachers' guides and supporting classroom materials—e.g., photographs and charts; but the emphasis is upon active learning with the details to be worked out by each teacher with his or her classes. The curriculum plan itself is clearly written and quite detailed. Each unit of study provides goals, behavioral objectives, concepts, and content. There is little reason for teachers to doubt what must be taught. It is their task to devise how best to teach the units to their pupils.

The new primary school curriculum attempts to resolve the problems identified by the various ministerial committees referred to earlier. There is far less emphasis upon academic subjects; the focus is on the children's own life experience. The overarching goal is to promote individual, community, and national development. The teacher is no longer required to follow blindly the national educational plans; rather, teachers have considerable freedom to adapt programs to local conditions. The use of community resources is encouraged, together with much greater emphasis upon active learning. The importance of competitive examinations has been reduced.[20]

Secondary School Reforms. The secondary curriculum has also changed markedly.[21] The two separate programs for "general" and "vocational" students have been abolished and replaced with a single program offering both general academic courses and vocational skill training. Students are able to follow a program of study suitable to their abilities and interests. At each higher grade there is an increasing emphasis upon practical and manual activities. This stems from a recognition that school must be concerned with more than the cognitive and affective growth of youth; school must also prepare youth for jobs.

The new secondary curriculum is divided into five semi-integrated areas: language, science and mathematics, social studies, character development, and work education. Within social studies, history and geography are no longer taught as separate subjects; rather they have become parts of more general courses about Thailand and other parts of the world. Courses are one-semester in length, with two required courses each year. There are no social studies electives at grades seven and eight. At grade nine students may choose two elective courses from among twelve that are offered. Examples of such electives are "Thai Society and Culture," "Lives and Works of Great Persons," "General Economics," "Law in Daily Life," "Environmental Studies and Conservation," "Population Education," "Elementary Geography," and "Thai History." The required courses for grades seven, eight and nine are: grade 7—"Our Country I and II"; grade 8—"Our Neighbors I and II"; grade 9—"Our World I and II." Each course runs one semester. Each course meets five periods each week.

The most striking changes in the new social studies program, compared to the curriculum it replaced in both the elementary and secondary schools, are the efforts to integrate knowledge from various disciplines, especially in the primary grades; the emphasis on making instruction relevant to the learner's own life and experience; the de-emphasis upon academic subject knowledge; and the concentration on thinking skills and problem-solving methods as being critically important in the preparation of effective citizens.

WHAT IS THE RELATIONSHIP BETWEEN SOCIAL STUDIES AND CITIZENSHIP EDUCATION?

The term "citizenship education" is not used in Thailand. However, the idea behind the term—i.e., education should prepare youth for effective citizenship—is widely accepted. Probably, most people would agree that a "good Thai citizen" is one (1) who possesses a sense of civic duty; (2) who respects the rights of others; (3) who supports and participates in a democratic government with the King as Head of State; and (4) who appreciates Thai culture.

Although social studies has accepted objectives that would presumably contribute to the development of such "good citizens," in the past little effort was made to achieve them. The content of social studies courses was too abstract and linked too closely to the academic disciplines to be very helpful in promoting citizenship education. Moreover, it has been widely assumed that formal education as a whole contributed to citizen development and that this was not a responsibility of social studies exclu-

One aspect of good citizenship is paying respect to teachers. Each year, a special day is set aside for students to pay homage to their teachers. Students prepare flower arrangements; classes compete with one another for prizes. In this picture, students are placing flowers before their teachers, who are seated outside of the range of the camera.

sively. Furthermore, character education, an important aspect of citizenship education, has been more closely linked to religious education and set aside from the secular studies that characterized the social studies.

Moreover, it is generally agreed that whether or not one becomes a "good citizen" depends as much or more upon a general pattern of socialization of which the school may play only a minor role. The family, peer groups, and the work place may have greater influence than the school.

Nevertheless, under the most recent curriculum reform, social studies teachers have been given greater responsibility for citizenship education because only the study of the Thai language and social studies are continuously required of all students. While citizenship education has not been listed as the central goal of social studies, of the six main goals of secondary school social studies, the first is to promote good citizenship in a democratic society with the King as Head of State. It is increasingly important for social studies teachers to contribute to the preparation of Thai youth for effective citizenship.

WHAT ARE THE MAJOR ISSUES IN THE SOCIAL STUDIES IN THAILAND?

Thailand is a developing nation, facing many complex social and economic problems. Social studies must somehow contribute to the nation's efforts to solve these problems. In the meantime, social studies instruction has problems of its own that must be resolved.

Confusion Over Goals. As noted previously, many primary school teachers have not understood the purposes of social studies. This has often led to aimless instruction in which teachers merely follow the textbooks and the lesson plans in a thoughtless manner.

Furthermore, criteria used for determining success in education have contributed to confusion. Social studies teachers accept broadly stated goals about the purposes of social studies and then act as if there were only one purpose: to stuff their students' heads with as much academic knowledge as possible. It is not surprising that this would occur. High school graduates have only a limited choice of good jobs. The best positions are reserved for college graduates. In order to attend college, high school graduates must receive a high score on competitive examinations. (According to the Fourth National Development Plan, 6,952,835 high school graduates will compete for only 195,345 slots available in universities.)[22] In order to help their students perform successfully on such examinations, social studies teachers emphasize academic knowledge and ignore more general social studies purposes. Students understand clearly what the educational system values. On the written examination, civics and ethics share only twenty points out of a possible score of 1000. This contributes to the second problem.

Status of Social Studies. Social studies is viewed as inferior to other school subjects, such as mathematics, science, and English. The best students are often advised to major in subjects other than social studies. Students who major in the social studies are generally viewed as the least able, those who are unable to succeed in more difficult subjects. There is some truth in this belief because social studies has typically emphasized rote memorization, rather than problem solving, creative thinking, and conceptualization. Social studies majors may have the best cultivated memories.

Moreover, social studies teachers often hold the subject in low esteem. They feel inferior to mathematics teachers, for example. Many social studies teachers were themselves less able students who would have preferred a different career had it been possible.

Social studies is less important in obtaining a good job when compared to other subjects. A student who is good in science, mathematics, or English has greater job opportunities and more choices in higher education.

Methods of Teaching Social Studies. Social studies teachers in Thailand depend too heavily upon lectures and textbooks. They confine instruction to the classroom and do little to encourage thinking or active involvement in learning. Moreover, the atmosphere in most classrooms does little to encourage imagination and creativity. Social studies classrooms are rather sober places. Students sense the power teachers have over them and do not experience close, friendly relations.

The new curriculum program intends to alter these conditions. Teachers will be asked to employ new methods and approaches. Furthermore, teachers will be asked to integrate knowledge in ways unfamiliar to them. Unfortunately, Thai teachers have not been trained according to the new expectations.[23] Newly graduated teachers in the social sciences have shown no greater competence in the new teaching approaches than the older teachers. Perhaps this is because typical student-teachers must enroll in only one course in teaching methods while they teach eight to ten courses in their subject specialty. Moreover, most of the courses in teacher colleges employ lectures almost exclusively. Therefore, student-teachers do not have good instructional models.

Status of Thai Culture. M. R. Kukrit Pramoj states in "Education and Culture"[24] that Thai culture today is in a state of utter confusion. Two main reasons are given: (1) Through technological assistance and other programs, Thailand has adapted Western civilization; and (2) Thai people have ignored their own culture for a very long time. For nearly a century, English and social studies teachers have been busily introducing their students to a foreign culture while neglecting their own. Foreign studies took precedence over local and national studies. It is not uncommon to see Thai youth with long hair, playing guitars or listening to jazz, who know nothing about "Khon" or "la-korn" (forms of Thai classical arts). Western materialism is a corrosive influence. Many Thai people respect its values and view their own culture as useless and outdated.

Social studies teachers must begin to approach the study of foreign cultures in a critical way. Students must evaluate ideas and practices from the West before adopting them or adapting them to Thai culture if this is necessary. At the same time, Thai culture must be appraised, preserving the good aspects and discarding those features that seem less essential for the present day. To preserve Thai culture only because it is indigenous to Thailand is not sufficient justification.

Conclusion

Thailand's social studies program shows unmistakable traces of the impact of social studies ideas from the United States and other Western nations. Yet social studies as practiced in Thailand rests squarely on Thai traditions, values, and perspectives. The changes that have been introduced recently, it is hoped, will prepare Thai people to cope even more successfully in the future with the problems facing our complex world.

NOTES

[1]See Department of Elementary and Adult Education, Ministry of Education, *Education in Thailand: A Century of Experience.* Bangkok, Thailand: Karnsasana Press, 1970, pp. 1–2. This publication discusses important events that influenced the development of Thai education from 1824 to 1916.

[2]Department of Educational Techniques, Ministry of Education, *Kwam Pen Ma Khong Uhaksut Saman Suksa (The Story of General Education Curriculum).* Bangkok, Thailand: Songserm Archeep Press, 1961, pp. 141–168. One chapter describes the development of social studies curriculum from its birth until the 1960 curriculum.

[3]*Education in Thailand: A Century of Experience, op. cit.,* p. 132.

[4]*Kwam Pen Ma Khong Uhaksut Saman Suksa, op. cit.,* pp. 158–166.

[5]*Kwam Pen Ma Khong Uhaksut Saman Suksa, op. cit.,* pp. 188–212. The chapter provides an insightful analysis of general education curriculum, 1960.

[6]Ministry of Education, *Phaen Karn Suksa Haeng Chart B.E. 2503 (The National Scheme of Education, 1960).* The scheme states educational goals, educational policies, and educational system of Thailand.

[7]For completely detailed syllabus and specific subject objectives in the four booklets of syllabus for lower and upper elementary and secondary education, see *ibid.*

[8]The International Institute for Child Studies and Department of General Education, *Rai Ngan Karn Wijai Lhuksut Prathom Suksa Ton Ton (Research on Lower Elementary Curriculum Analysis).* Bangkok, Thailand: Kurusabha Press, 1966, pp. 197–202.

[9]*Education in Thailand: A Century of Experience, op. cit.,* pp. 100–112.

[10]*Ibid.,* p. 137.

[11]Buabucha Suetrong, *Karn Wikroh Phrutikum Kiawkup Karn Chai Kan Phood Nai Karn Rian Karn Son (Analysis of Verbal Behavior in Teaching Learning Process).* Graduate School (Master's thesis). Chulalongkorn University, 1969. The sample was 112 students of grades 8–10 and 12 teachers of the demonstration school at Chulalongkorn University. Two of the findings were: lecturing is most often used by teachers, and teachers use verbal behavior more in social studies classes than in courses in mathematics and the Thai Language.

[12]*Education in Thailand: A Century of Experience, op. cit.,* p. 114. The value of schooling for the purpose of government employment has been popular and is deeply rooted among Thai people.

[13]Civics and ethics instruction has been neglected and is viewed as outdated. The content of these courses, especially ethics, is not relevant to the children's lives. The methods employed in teaching make it additionally boring.

[14]The most serious problem about textbooks and materials is their scarcity. In some remote areas, less than 10% of pupils have the required texts and access to a library. As for the implementation of the new curriculum, the Ministry realizes the problems and is making extra effort to provide textbooks for all children in required schooling.

[15]Schools and teachers gain prestige when their students succeed in competition for places in prestigious colleges or universities, or when their students appear among the top ten of all high school graduates throughout the country. In the future, rigid national controls for evaluating the final high-school grade will no longer exist. Evaluation will be each teacher's responsibility.

[16]Department of Educational Techniques, Ministry of Education, *Rai Ngan Karn Wichroh Lhuksut Phrathom Suksa B.E. 2503 (Report on the National Primary Curriculum 1960 Analysis).* Bangkok, Thailand: Khurusabha Press, 1974, pp. 23–27.

[17]*Ibid.,* pp. 48, 53, 65–66, 69.

[18]The National Council, *Warasarn Sabha Karn Suksa Haeng Chart (Development of the National Scheme of Education). Journal of the National Education Council.* Vol. 4 (April–May, 1977), pp. 123–139.

[19]Decentralization is a trend in the Thai educational system. Local authorities are encouraged to participate in the improvement of curriculum and in preparing texts and other materials. Moreover, each region is allowed to teach local customs, religion, occupations, etc.

[20]The main purpose of evaluation will no longer be for the selection of top students but for individual improvement.

[21]Ministry of Education, *Lhuksut Matayom Suksa Ton Ton (Lower Secondary Curriculum 1978).* Bangkok, Thailand: Jongjareon Press, 1977.

[22]The Ministry of Education, *The Fourth National Development Plan 1977–1981.* Bangkok, Thailand: Karnsasana Press, 1977, p. 4.

[23]Teacher competence is another problem for remote areas. Qualified teachers wish to work in urban areas because of the lack of facilities, poor living conditions, and communist terrorists in more remote spots. In 1978, 12,000 applicants competed for 2,000 positions in governmental secondary schools in the Bangkok metropolitan area, while less than the number needed applied for schools in rural areas.

[24]*Education in Thailand: A Century of Experience, op. cit.,* pp. 38–52.

Social Studies in Japan

Jiro Nagai

WHAT DOES SOCIAL STUDIES MEAN IN JAPAN?

Social studies became a school subject through the enforcement regulations of the school education law promulgated by the Japanese government in 1947.[1] After the surrender ending World War II, Japan adopted many features of American education. This was accomplished under the strong leadership of the allied forces which occupied Japan for about six years after the war. The Japanese government tried to remove Japanese militarism and ultra-nationalism and to reconstruct Japan as a peaceful and democratic nation. It took some initiative in revising the traditional school curricula, which had been strongly influenced by European education. History, geography, and civics were separate and independent subjects at elementary and secondary levels. The allies suggested that the integrated social studies in the American pattern might be best suited for the democratization of Japanese society. Thus, social studies appeared in the school curricula of elementary and secondary levels.

Unfortunately, most Japanese teachers were not familiar with the new curriculum and did not understand what social studies entailed. They were quite at a loss in teaching it. Much criticism was directed against social studies by Japanese educators, historians, and the general public.

Since that time, especially after the independence of Japan, the government has endeavored to take into consideration both the reality of Japanese society and the desires of the Japanese people. It has especially endeavored to promote pupils' understanding of Japan; that is, of Japanese history, geography, morality, and values.

In Japan, the basic principles for curricula in elementary and secondary schools are prescribed by the Ministry of Education through the enforcement regulations of the school education law. The standards of curriculum organization, the objectives, and the content of each subject are established and made public as "courses of study" for each school level. Each school is required to organize a suitable curriculum for its specific conditions in accordance with the governing regulations and courses of study. The curriculum is then subject to the approval of the local board of education.

The course of study for social studies has been revised by the Ministry several times during the last thirty years. In general, Japanese social studies has developed through four stages. During the first stage, immediately after World War II, Japan imported and imitated faithfully American social studies. In the second stage, during the 1950s, Japan endeavored to revise the imported social studies to consider the real situation in Japan. During the 1960s, the third stage, Japanese social studies became comparatively stable and better suited to the reality of modern Japan. The current course of study for social studies in elementary and secondary levels was established in the later 1960s. Now underway is a fourth stage; social studies is being revised again both theoretically and practically under the new wave of educational innovation developing in many countries of the world. Many new ideas, such as the new social studies (USA), *Gemeinschaftskunde* or *Gesellschaftslehre* (West Germany), and modern studies or general studies (Britain), are influencing this latest revision of social studies education in Japan.

Formally, social studies is thought to be a subject integrating history, geography, and civics under problem-solving units, putting importance on pupils' lives and experiences. In reality, however, its segmentation has been increased with every revised course of study. Therefore, the present social studies in Japan can be said to consist of three main fields: history, geography, and civics. Initially, moral education was included in the social studies. Since the 1958 revision of school curricula, however, moral education has been separated from social studies and has become an important area of the school curriculum, especially at elementary and lower secondary levels.

The Present Course of Study for Social Studies[2]

Elementary and Lower Secondary. In Japan, an elementary school education of six years and a lower secondary school education of three years are both compulsory. Social studies courses are required at all levels. Based on the 1968 course of study, the general objective of elementary social studies is: "To guide children to deepen their grasp of social life and enable them to cultivate the foundation of citizenship so that they may live as members of a democratic nation and society."[3]

First graders learn about their immediate social life, such as the school, the home, and the neighborhood. Second graders learn about the function of retail stores and about people who are engaged in the cultivation of farm products, the promotion of forestry resources, and the fishing industry. They also learn about the work of people in factories, in transportation (such as railways and buses), in the post office, and in police and fire stations. Third graders learn about community life in their own city, town, or village, the function of local government, historical changes as reflected in the lives of people in their neighborhood, and the achievements of their ancestors. Fourth graders study the lives of the people in their own political district and broader areas. Fifth-grade students learn about the geography of Japan and the historical background of modern Japanese industry. Those at the sixth-grade level learn about the history

Sixth graders are learning about one period in the ancient times of Japan. A boy is describing a Buddha image.

Fourth graders are learning the geographical features of their prefecture. A girl is asking her classmates to respond to her oral report.

of Japan, the Japanese constitution, the function of Japanese government, and some world geography.

Elementary social studies has still maintained a feature of content integration, although some differentiation appears in the upper grades.

The general objective of lower secondary (junior high school) social studies is stated in the present course of study, established in 1969, as follows: "Through studies of geography, history, politics, economy, and social affairs, the pupils are to acquire an understanding of social life and to establish the foundation for qualities essential to the members of a democratic and peaceful nation."[4]

Seventh graders are learning about Japanese industry. A student is preparing the overhead projector for his oral report.

Social studies in the lower secondary school consists of three fields: geography, history, and civics. In geography, the proportion of Japanese geography to world geography is approximately equal. In history, however, the proportion of Japanese history to world history is about 70/30. The field of civics has social, economic, and political content. Here the pupils learn about family life, social life, economics, and politics, with an emphasis on understanding the Japanese constitution.

Ordinarily, geography and history are taught concurrently in the seventh and eighth grades. Contemporary history is taught from the beginning of the ninth grade. In considering the actual conditions in school, geography may be completed in the seventh grade. In such a case, history can be taught in the eighth grade. Civics must be taken in the ninth grade, which is the final year of compulsory education in Japan, on the completion of both geography and history. The structure of these three fields is illustrated in Figure 1.

Figure 1: Social Studies in Lower Secondary School

9th grade	*Field of Civics* 140 school hours (4 hours per week)
	(Contemporary History) 35 school hours
8th grade	*Field of Geography* 70 school hours (2 hours per week) / *Field of History* 70 school hours (2 hours per week)
7th grade	70 school hours (2 hours per week) / 70 school hours (2 hours per week)

Upper Secondary. The general objective of upper secondary (senior high school) social studies is stated in the 1970 course of study: "The pupils are to deepen their understanding and awareness of social life and to develop those qualities which are essential for building a democratic and peaceful society."[5] The structure of upper secondary social studies is diagrammed in Figure 2.

Tenth graders are studying geography. A boy and a girl are cooperating in their oral report on world climate, using the overhead projector.

Figure 2: Social Studies in Upper Secondary School

Ethics-Sociology	(2 credits)	11th or 12th grade, or through 11th and 12th grade
Politics-Economics	(2 credits)	As above.
Japanese History	(3 credits)	As above.
World History	(3 credits)	10th or 11th grade, or through 10th and 11th grade
Geography A	(3 credits)	As above.
Geography B	(3 credits)	As above.

*Note: Geography A is systematic geography, and Geography B is world topography. The number of credits is standard. A credit means one school hour (50 minutes) per week.

Ethics-sociology and politics-economics are required subjects. Japanese history, world history, geography A, and geography B are all elective, but pupils must select two of them. In the general course, it is recommended as desirable that pupils learn all five subjects; that is, ethics-sociology, politics-economics, Japanese history, world history, and geography A or geography B.

Upper secondary school education is not compulsory, even though more than 90 percent of the graduates from the lower secondary advance to the upper secondary. The curriculum of the upper secondary school has more differentiation than that of the elementary and lower secondary schools. And there is more variation in curricula, which include full-time, part-time, and correspondence programs, and general and vocational programs.

Textbooks. In Japan, every textbook used in elementary and secondary schools must follow the course of study promulgated by the Ministry of Education and must also be approved by the Ministry. Every local board of education appoints a special committee of teachers to select textbooks for each subject for use in their school district. There is some variety in textbooks and in teaching practices. Classroom teachers have freedom to select methods of teaching and to develop teaching materials other than textbooks.

WHAT IS THE RELATIONSHIP BETWEEN
SOCIAL STUDIES AND CITIZENSHIP EDUCATION?

As the course of study of lower secondary social studies states, Japanese social studies aims to foster an understanding and cognizance of social life and establish a foundation for qualities essential to members of a democratic and peaceful nation and society. The essential aim of social studies instruction has two aspects: one is to build up students' scientific awareness of society; the other is to develop students as citizens for a democratic society. Thus, social studies is a curriculum subject for promoting citizenship by fostering a scientific awareness of society. In this sense, social studies instruction in Japan contributes much to the development of citizenship in the Japanese people.

Regarding the content of citizenship, it is expected in Japan that a good citizen should:

1. realize that the dignity of the individual and respect for human rights form the basis of a democratic social life;

2. have a deep love and awareness of his or her own nation and culture and have a willingness to contribute to their advancement; and

3. have a spirit of international understanding and cooperation, and an attitude of making contributions to world peace and the welfare of humankind.

In sum, being a good Japanese means being a democratic and world-minded citizen with a relevant, deep national consciousness.

Moral Education. Although there is no specific moral education in the upper secondary school, it is an important and independent area of the school curriculum at elementary and lower secondary levels. Moral education is also much concerned with citizen education.[6]

The present courses of study for moral education in elementary and lower secondary schools in Japan recommend that: "Moral education should be carried out as to be basic to all the educational activities of the school. Therefore, proper instruction should be given not only during moral education, but also during each subject and special activity in conformance with their respective characteristics."[7]

The main objectives of moral education are to foster in the students the moral character essential to their upbringing, to put into practice the spirit of respect for human beings in the students' actual lives in their homes, schools, and in other societies, to strive for the creation of a culture rich in individuality, to develop a democratic society and state, and to contribute to the realization of a peaceful international society.

The content of moral education contains several items conducive to good citizenship. For example, moral education in the lower secondary school includes the following:

Students should endeavor to respect life, promote mental and physical well-being, and acquire the proper modes of everyday behavior. They should make their own decisions and assume responsibility for the consequences. Students should respect the different ideas and positions of others and thus learn in a climate of mutual trust and should develop the desire to continue learning and aim at achieving their fullest potential. They should function harmoniously within society, in the spirit of law and order, being fully aware of both their duties and their rights. And lastly, they should strive to contribute toward world peace and the general welfare of humankind from a global perspective.[8]

It is easy to understand that moral education is closely related to citizenship education. Some people, however, criticize this kind of moral education as not being moral in the true sense, but being an idealistic list-of-virtues approach. This is one of the reasons why teachers think this is a difficult area with which to deal.[9]

Regardless, moral education aims at supplementing, deepening, and integrating the moral virtues in the other educational activities and subjects. The objective is to have students develop an understanding of humanity, enhance their ability to make moral judgments, and enrich their moral sense.

Social studies has both cognitive and affective dimensions. The affective domain contains moral attitudes as well as citizenship. Therefore, social studies should stress both moral and citizenship education. However, the primary objective of social studies is to give students an understanding of society, and to back up their desirable attitudes by establishing a firm foundation of correct moral decisions. The aim of moral education is to internalize and deepen these attitudes and sense of morality in accordance with the student's individuality and immediate environment. Therefore, social studies should build up the bases of the instruction given in moral education, making it more concrete and practical, while the latter should deepen the abilities of moral decision-making developed by social studies.

Social studies and moral education coordinate with one another to develop students' morality as well as their citizenship. In this sense, both social studies and moral education are playing very important roles in promoting citizen education in Japan.

WHAT ARE THE MAJOR ISSUES
IN THE SOCIAL STUDIES IN JAPAN?

Curriculum Revision. The Council for School Curriculum, which is an important advisory committee of the Ministry of Education in Japan, presented a report in 1976 on the necessity of revising school curricula. Taking this report into consideration, the Ministry is now proceeding with the revision. The new elementary and lower secondary curricula were announced in July 1977. The newly revised courses of study will be enforced by the Ministry in two or three years' time. The new course of study for upper secondary schools was also announced in 1978. It will be enforced four years later.

The present curricula for the elementary and secondary schools have been criticized by parents and educators alike as difficult and overloaded. The main criticism is that they are designed to cram too much too soon into the heads of the youngsters. The new curricula embody quantitative and qualitative revisions of the present versions. In terms of quantity, the new curriculum standards propose to reduce the burden of school work by decreasing the number of class hours by almost ten percent. In terms of quality, the content of each subject would be slightly reduced and made more understandable through the careful selection of more effective teaching materials.

So far as social studies is concerned, the structure, content, and objectives have not been changed significantly. Yet, some innovations have been introduced. For example, rigid distinction between the scope of local community as learned by the third graders and that learned by the fourth graders has been removed. Another example is that the content of world geography in the sixth grade has been moved to the seventh grade (the first year of the lower secondary school).

The content of the field of civics in the ninth grade (the third year of the lower secondary school) also has been rearranged. It takes into consideration the content of a new subject called "contemporary society," which has appeared as a required subject in the tenth grade (the first year of the upper secondary school). This new subject is a comprehensive social studies which integrates ethics, politics, and economics; it is mainly concerned with contemporary society and recurring social problems.

The distinction between geography A and B has been abolished, unifying both as "geography." As "contemporary society" is a required subject in the tenth grade, other subjects such as Japanese history, world history, geography, ethics, and politics-economics have all become electives in the eleventh and twelfth grades.

Teaching Strategies. One of the up-to-date issues of school education in Japan is how to adapt teaching situations to these new courses of study. All of the textbooks are now being revised by the respective publishers. In this sense, Japanese school education is in a transition today. Relating to this new trend, an interesting survey about problems in social studies instruction was carried out at the annual national meeting of the Japan Social Studies Research Association, held at Shimane University, November 1977. Participants at the meeting were requested to present their own concerns and opinions about serious problems needing solution in social studies education. In this investigation, many issues (more than thirty items) were raised.

Among them, the following ten were thought by the respondents to be most important.

1. How should the pupils' scientific awareness of society be developed?
2. How should one organize a viewpoint or a framework, in order to select content of instruction?
3. How should the community approach be taken in developing teaching materials?
4. What is the relationship between social studies and the social sciences?
5. How can social studies lessons be made more understandable for the pupils?
6. What analytical questions should be used in social studies teaching?
7. Problems in the recently revised curriculum of social studies.
8. The meaning of attainment in learning.

9. Humanization of social studies instruction.
10. Individualization of social studies instruction.

In addition to these issues of curriculum revision and teaching strategies, this author would like to mention specifically the necessity of an interdisciplinary approach and an international/global approach for social studies education as urgent key issues to be considered.

Interdisciplinary Approach. As mentioned before, the lower secondary social studies consists of three fields: geography, history, and civics. The upper secondary social studies has even more separation. There is a serious problem as to how well students can understand the society with this kind of separation. In reality, historical, geographical, political, economic, and cultural elements are mixed and integrated in concrete social phenomena. It is absolutely necessary to approach social phenomena with synthetic and comprehensive points of view. Furthermore, citizenship itself is a synthetic and integrated component with various kinds of constituents.

Therefore, a more comprehensive and integrated approach should be taken in Japanese social studies education. This requires some kind of interdisciplinary approach. This is one of the reasons why a new course, "contemporary society," with integrated content has been introduced at the upper secondary level, as mentioned above.

Global Education. Educators are now being confronted with many difficult problems involving the environment, population, food, natural resources, human welfare, nuclear weapons, war, and peace. These problems cannot be solved without international cooperation on a global scale. Most contemporary issues involve international relations. The present world is shrinking rapidly due to the development of scientific technology; interdependence among nations is being strengthened day-by-day. The welfare and development of one nation cannot be attained solely from within its own territory; they are related to the problems shared by all humankind. Therefore, international understanding and cooperation among the nations of the world are needed more and more for the solution of these problems. Today, international awareness, world-mindedness, and global viewpoints have become necessary for the livelihood of every nation. In this sense, international education or global education must be given increased emphasis in social studies education. It may be said that social studies education for the twenty-first century should be international/global education.[10]

The Importance of Global Education for Japan. In 1974, the Central Council for Education presented the Minister of Education with a report entitled "On International Exchange of Education, Science, and Culture," which emphasized international cooperation in these fields. The report stressed the importance of developing education for international understanding and of improving international exchange activities in education, science, and culture in order to educate the Japanese people so that they will be more active in, and make a greater contribution toward, international society. It notes that while Japan has endeavored to import modern knowledge and skills from America and European countries, it has neglected to develop a comprehensive understanding of these countries. On the other hand, the report recognizes that Japan has tried to assimilate positive aspects of Western civilization and to build a modern nation during this century. It also notes, however, that Japan has failed to help other countries understand her better.

Japan has been criticized for immaturity in attitudes concerning international cooperation. This, of course, is due to geographical location and a lack of strong contact with other nations and cultures in daily life. This underlies the foreign misunderstanding and mistrust of Japan and of its people in recent years, as the Japanese have become very active abroad. It is, therefore, necessary for Japanese people to improve their international attitudes. Moreover, the world is now confronted with various problems that demand more understanding and cooperation in order to be resolved. It is thus the duty of the Japanese people to develop mutual understanding with other peoples, building up world-mindedness and an active desire to improve relations with others. Accordingly, it is also the duty of social studies instruction for Japanese citizenship to promote international/intercultural/global education.

Rapid Growth and Professional Diversity. In the past thirty years, the study of social studies education has developed greatly in Japan. Every revision of the course of study raised many problems and engendered much discussion. The teaching practices of social studies also have been advanced. Many books, educational magazines, and various other kinds of teaching materials and publications on social studies education in Japan have been published. There are a number of university scholars who specialize in studying social studies education. Every teacher training college or university has its own division of social studies education.

There are many local and national professional associations and societies. Many of these have their own interpretations of social studies. Some of them place importance on history and geography, some on other social sciences, and some others on the problem-solving social studies which stresses pupils' lives, experiences, and activities. From its leftist ideology, the teachers' union of Japan always criticizes the course of study announced by the Ministry of Education. Other associations have a more academic, objective, and scientific viewpoint. Two of these are the Japan Social Studies Research Association and the Japan Society for Social Studies Education.

Conclusion

Today, the study of social studies education is being established as an important branch of education science. Yet, people are still asking what is social studies education? What are its inherent aims or objectives? What should be its proper content? What are its best methods? Correct answers to these questions will be determined by developing a specialized and scientific curriculum study of social studies education. Consequently, it may be another important issue of social studies instruction in Japan to establish more firmly the research on social studies education as an educational science.

NOTES

[1]More elaborate descriptions of this argument can be found in Itsuo Okabe, "The Evolution of Social Studies in the Elementary School," *Education in Japan–Journal for Overseas,* Vol. III, The International Education Research Institute, Hiroshima University, 1968, pp. 25–33, and Iwao Utsumi, "The Development of Social Studies in the Secondary Schools," *Education in Japan—Journal for Overseas,* Vol. IV, 1969, pp. 41–51.

[2]Ronald S. Anderson, *Education in Japan—A Century of Modern Development,* U.S. Department of Health, Education, and Welfare, Office of Education, 1975, pp. 117–119 (Elementary), pp. 128–130 (Junior High), pp. 168–170 (Senior High).

[3]Educational and Cultural Exchange Division, Science and International Affairs Bureau, Ministry of Education, Science and Culture, *Course of Study for Elementary Schools in Japan,* Ministry of Education, 1976, pp. 31–57 (Social Studies).

[4]Educational and Cultural Exchange Division, Science and International Affairs Bureau, Ministry of Education, Science and Culture, *Course of Study for Lower Secondary Schools in Japan,* 1976, pp. 20–57 (Social Studies).

[5]Educational and Cultural Exchange Division, Science and International Affairs Bureau, Ministry of Education, Science and Culture, *Course of Study for Upper Secondary Schools in Japan,* 1976, pp. 35–61 (Social Studies).

[6]Byron G. Massialas discussed the relationship between social studies and moral education in Japan in *New Challenges in the Social Studies—Implications of Research for Teaching,* Wadsworth Publishing Company, Inc., 1965, pp. 200–203.

[7]*Course of Study for Elementary Schools in Japan, op. cit.,* pp. 200–205 (moral education).

[8]*Course of Study for Lower Secondary Schools in Japan, op. cit.,* pp. 235–239 (moral education).

[9]Ronald S. Anderson discussed problems of moral education in Japan, *op. cit.,* pp. 113–117 (Elementary), pp. 135–140 (Junior High).

[10]Jiro Nagai, "The Theory of Education for International Understanding," *Bulletin of the Faculty of Education, Hiroshima University,* Part 1, No. 24, Hiroshima University, 1975, pp. 143–157. Jiro Nagai, "Recent Developments of Education for International Understanding," *Bulletin of the Faculty of Education, Hiroshima University,* Part 1, No. 25, Hiroshima University, 1976, pp. 151–161.

Social Studies in Nigeria

Vincent O. Onyabe

WHAT DOES SOCIAL STUDIES MEAN IN NIGERIA?

Good education changes as the cultural, social, economic, and political needs of the society for which it was designed change. But because every change involves some risk, it takes some time for changes to establish themselves and to become accepted as desirable innovations. How people conceive the meaning and function of a new aspect of the curriculum will be greatly influenced by both the circumstances that led to the introduction of this change and the social and economic resources available for its promotion. The case of social studies in Nigeria has not been different. This chapter shall outline the development of social studies in Nigeria and discuss the problems of its promotion with a view to assessing its present and future roles in the educational system of this country.

Social Studies Since Independence. Up to and after the attainment of independence in 1960, schools in Nigeria taught traditional, separate, and unintegrated geography and history at all levels of the educational system. Geography featured specifically the learning of definitions and of landforms, place names, and economic activities in foreign lands. History was characterized by learning the biographies of foreign heroes and heroines. A catalogue of events and dates provided by the teacher was committed to memory by students for ready recitation.

Soon after independence there were signs of awareness here and there that the social education provided in schools was unsuitable. Examination results were poor. Research conducted among secondary school students showed that geography and history were among the most unpopular subjects. Although these revelations did not give rise to direct curriculum change in geography and history, they formed part of the general concern that prepared the way for the now famous national curriculum conference of 1969 held in Lagos.

Curriculum Changes. The national curriculum conference, organised by the National Education Research Council (NERC) nine years after independence, was unique in that it was the first time in the history of this

Above. *A Nigerian cattle herder.*
Below. *Transporting people and goods across Lake Chad.*

country that Nigerians by themselves were setting educational objectives for their own children. Three statements of belief about the role of Nigerian education emerged from the conference. These were:

1. the belief in the worth of the individual and the development of all Nigerian children for each individual's sake and for the development of society in general;
2. the belief in providing Nigerian children with equal educational opportunity so that they can develop according to their ability; and
3. the belief in a functional type of education that will facilitate democracy as a way of life, and promote the development of an effective, informed Nigerian citizenry.[1]

Teacher Training. The first efforts to change the nature and content of social education in Nigeria came from outside. Even before the 1969 national curriculum conference, the Ford Foundation had plans to introduce social studies into the Nigeria school curriculum. In the early 1960s, the Ford Foundation, working through the University of Washington, began curriculum development in social studies at the Aiyetoro Comprehensive High School in Western Nigeria.[2] About the same time, the Foundation, working through the University of Wisconsin, in collaboration with the then Northern Nigerian government, launched a program in Northern Nigeria to improve primary school teacher preparation. This project covered five subject areas, including social studies. While the two projects produced useful materials for the promotion of social studies, social studies did not make an inroad into the Nigerian educational system until the early 1970s. The reluctance and uncertainty of teachers about social studies were such that the excellent social studies methods book, the first of its type in this country, had to be titled "Geography and History Methods"[3] to make it acceptable.

By 1970, it became obvious that if the noble objectives set in 1969 were to be achieved, integrated social studies, in place of the traditional geography and history, must be encouraged. In 1971, the Nigeria Educational Research Council, on behalf of the Federal government, organised a workshop to draft a national syllabus in social studies.[4] A similar exercise produced the post-primary syllabus in 1974.[5] This action, and financial support given to social studies programs by the Federal government, indicates that the government has accepted social studies as desirable social education for the nation.

With Federal government encouragement and efforts by the Institute of Education and the Department of Education of Ahmadu Bello University, social studies has replaced traditional geography and history in all primary schools in the country.[6] Most post-primary institutions now teach social studies in the first two years. Ahmadu Bello University offers degree and diploma courses in social studies education.

Differing Beliefs About Social Studies. The tremendous progress reported above has been made over a short period of time. Social studies as a formal school subject in Nigeria is only fifteen years old. It is, therefore, a new subject area to many people in the Nigerian society. Different meanings are thus accorded social studies by different groups in Nigeria. One could identify four main groups of people whose views are important to the development of social studies:

1. people with training in social studies;
2. tutors in post-primary institutions;
3. primary school teachers; and
4. top officials of the state ministries of education.

Among the few people in Nigeria with formal training in social studies education, social studies is considered an applied field of study that employs the key concepts of the social sciences to help children improve through investigation their understanding of the world in which they live. This group of people can no longer be satisfied with schools and teachers who do not encourage children to think for themselves, identify problems, attempt to find solutions, and evaluate new situations as they arise. They see content, or acquisition of factual knowledge, as a mere vehicle used to help students develop the basic skills, attitudes, and values.

Post-primary institutions in Nigeria include secondary schools, grade II teachers' colleges, commercial colleges, and technical colleges. Most of the people who teach here hold either the first university degree (with or without professional teaching qualifications) or the National Certificate in Education (NCE). It is not an overstatement to note that the greatest opposition to social studies education comes from this category of teachers. Two reasons seem to support this assessment: 1. The graduate teachers or the NCE holders major in specific subjects in their training. They see themselves as specialists and would like to be identified as such: either as historians, geographers, or political scientists, as the case may be. They, therefore, regard the teaching of social studies as a synthetic field—something that lowers their prestige. 2. Until Ahmadu Bello University began to offer in-service and degree courses in social studies, no university or advanced teachers college offered courses in social studies education.

The average primary school teacher in Nigeria has five years of post-primary education with a bias towards classroom teaching. The curriculum of teacher training colleges includes the content and methodology of all the primary school subjects. The primary teacher is, therefore, a generalist and sees his or her role as that of a facilitator of a program, not its initiator. Primary teachers are trained in traditional geography and history. The primary school teacher, with no previous exposure to social studies methodology, perceives social studies as a new subject—some combination of geography and history introduced by the government, for reasons best known to it and for which there has been no preparation. But the primary teacher obediently teaches social studies to stay employed.

The fourth group of people whose views of social studies are important to its development are officials of the various state ministries of education. They are charged with the responsibility of releasing money for in-service courses and the purchase of materials. Naturally, these people are at times reluctant to commit public funds to promote a subject which they little understand. To this class of people, social studies is a new subject that replaces history and geography in the school curriculum. In general, it is viewed as an added burden which calls for making money available to retrain teachers and to develop new materials.

Although social studies education has made significant progress in the past several years, much remains to be accomplished.

WHAT IS THE RELATIONSHIP BETWEEN SOCIAL STUDIES AND CITIZENSHIP EDUCATION?

Education, as a process through which the accumulated ideals cherished by the older generation are transmitted to the younger generation, must reflect the goals that the society has set for itself. Government identifies such goals for the people in the form of national policies. Nigeria is a developing nation of over 240 ethnic groups with a sad experience of a bloody civil war behind it. The Nigerian Federal government has set one major national objective: to promote national unity and to develop the economy for the benefit of all citizens.

Although the Federal government encourages development at the local and state levels, it has taken over the provision of major services, such as education, construction of major roads, supply and distribution of essential commodities, and price control services, in order to promote economic justice and evenly distributed development. Attendant to this effort are the Federal government's actions to remove individuals and groups which attempt to frustrate the creation of an egalitarian society. It comes as no surprise, therefore, that the Federal government has dismissed or retired public servants who were proven to be corrupt, indolent, unproductive, or undisciplined.

Several other recent moves have added weight to this policy. In 1975, the Federal government introduced the National Youth Corps scheme, under which all Nigerian youth graduating from universities or other institutions of higher learning serve a compulsory one-year term in states other than their own. The Federal government maintains that every Nigerian is entitled to a pensionable appointment in any part of the country.

The Universal Primary Education Scheme launched in 1976 was an attempt: (1) to put education within the reach of the poor, and (2) to correct the imbalance in education between the geographic areas which had an early start in educational development and those which were educationally undeveloped. National cultural and sports festivals, which the Federal government sponsors, bring Nigerians of diverse backgrounds together and help them to realize how much they have in common.

The most recent move at promoting national consciousness was made by the Head of State. He gave the Nation a pledge (p. 66) that school children are required to recite daily at school:

Social Studies Helps Children Learn About Their Environment Through Active Participation in the Learning Process

Above. *Children learn about the home as an institution of the nation.*
Below. *Through role playing, children learn to make their contribution to home management—the first step toward good citizenship.*

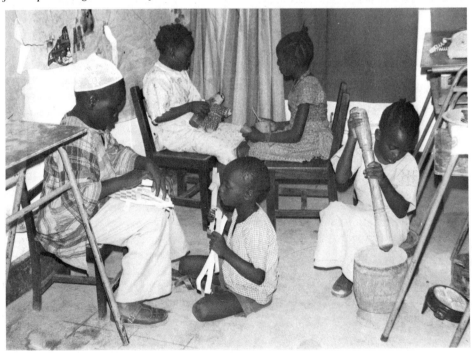

Above. *Social studies gives children the opportunity to enjoy themselves while they learn their cultural and national values through story-telling and singing.*
Below. *What is learned in school is consolidated through participation in the national community; members of the national youth service corps work on a rural development project.*

OUR PLEDGE
I pledge to Nigeria my country
to be faithful, loyal and honest
To serve Nigeria with all my strength
To defend her unity and uphold her honor
and glory, so help me God.

The government is aware that these noble objectives can only be achieved through an effective educational system. The Federal government's commitment to citizen education is reflected in the educational objectives it has set down for each level of the educational system.[7] These objectives are summarized below:

Primary Education: The objectives for primary education include the ability to communicate effectively, to think critically, to participate in the democratic process, and to pursue further educational advancement and self-improvement in a changing society.

Secondary Education: The objectives for secondary education reinforce the objectives for the elementary grades with the additional focus on the development of Nigerian culture, art, and languages and the ability to function effectively in a modern, technological society.

Teacher Education: Objectives for teacher education aim to produce motivated and efficient classroom teachers who encourage the spirit of inquiry and possess the ability to adapt to social change.

It may be concluded from these objectives that the government desires that the curricula of schools, at all levels, be Nigerian in orientation and that students and teachers be equipped to adapt to changes in society. They must be effective citizens; that is, they must be intellectually capable and versed in the skills of decision-making. It is obvious that the traditional geography and history curricula cannot contribute meaningfully to the attainment of these objectives. This seems to be why the Federal government has come out openly in support of integrated social studies.

In response to the aspirations of the Nigerian government, workshops organised by the Nigeria Education Research Council in 1971 and in 1974 set the following social studies objectives for the nation. These social studies objectives do not vary in essence from those general education objectives summarized above.

Objectives for social studies at the primary level stress resourcefulness, continued learning, a tolerance of others, and the willingness to accept necessary social change within a democratic framework.

The social studies objectives of post-primary education aim to develop an appreciation of Nigerian culture, an understanding of the evolving social and physical environment, and an awareness of the interdependence among people.

These objectives are reflected in the content of the National Syllabus, the major themes of which are presented in the appendix.

In order to ensure effective teaching of citizen education, teachers are urged to organise a current affairs lesson at least once a fortnight. This is in addition to the students reciting the national pledge daily and singing the national anthem in school at least twice weekly. It is recommended to teachers that the current affairs topics they select reflect the main theme of the syllabus for each respective class. For Primary One, accordingly, students are given the opportunity to report, discuss, and study simple events relating to their homes and their school. Primary Two focuses on events in the local community, while Primary Three mainly studies events in the local government area or the home district. For the senior primary classes, simple events and issues are similarly related to the themes of their syllabuses. In each case, examples of cooperation, selfless service, tolerance, philanthropy, objective reasoning, honesty, loyalty, patriotism, and other citizenship qualities are examined and challenged.

The teacher's role in citizenship education cannot be overemphasized. Social studies teachers are advised, through study guides and in-service courses, to avoid indoctrination, to be approachable, and to create a democratic classroom atmosphere in which children can feel free, within reasonable limits, to influence decisions on work selection, learning procedures, and evaluation of findings.

Not everyone in Nigeria is attuned to citizen education. In fact, it is safe to state that, while the government is highly committed to getting Nigerians to associate themselves with the national objectives and to defend them with pride, this zeal does not seem to be evenly diffused among the masses. The irony of this situation is that Nigeria, which desires and encourages the acquisition of social, moral, and religious values, administers an examination system which demands the regurgitation of isolated bodies of factual knowledge. It is generally accepted that examination systems influence how teachers teach and what students regard as worthwhile to know.

Fortunately, social studies in Nigeria, particularly at the primary and secondary levels, uses the interdisciplinary approach. In the primary and secondary programs, an elementary knowledge of sociology, economics, government, and civics (in addition to history and geography) is required in order to teach effectively. At Ahmadu Bello University, in addition to the educational courses common to all students, social studies students are required to take courses in economics, history, geography, political science, and sociology.

WHAT ARE THE MAJOR ISSUES IN THE SOCIAL STUDIES IN NIGERIA?

Social studies is gradually becoming an influential force in the Nigerian educational system. Yet, many problems must be solved before it can be established as a recognized field of study. However, social studies, with its new content and open approach, has caused concern and even doubt in the minds of many educators. Four major problems stand in the way of social studies education in Nigeria:

1. the contending position of social scientists and social studies educators;
2. the lack of a clear definition of standards for the social studies educator;
3. the force of tradition; and
4. inadequate resource materials.

Contending Positions. It is a paradox that one of the obstacles to promotion of social studies in Nigeria is the opposition of some social scientists. Social scientists are committed to widening knowledge in their areas of specialization. They tend to view integrated social studies as general education which lowers the standards in the traditional social sciences. Thus, those individuals in the best position to encourage social studies impede its development. Efforts are already underway to bridge this gap. For example, professional social studies organizations are encouraging social scientists to participate in social studies workshops, seminars, and in-service courses.

Lack of Clear Definition. As is the case in most nations of the world, there is little agreement on the philosophical conception of social studies. The unfortunate result is that traditional textbooks are reappearing under the new social studies label. This causes more confusion than guidance for teachers. The Nigeria Educational Research Council (NERC) has already taken a step in the right direction by encouraging teacher training colleges to use only the social studies books written by the special panels it has established. Eventually, the social studies bodies will have to address seriously the inevitable question, "What are the standards for the social studies educator in Nigeria?"

Tradition. Perhaps the greatest problem that confronts social studies is the obstacle of tradition. This affects the integrated program in two ways; it raises the questions of where to start instruction and what is the nature of teacher education.

The problem of deciding at what level to begin the social studies program has become the question of the egg and the chicken. The general consensus seems to support introducing social studies in the primary school. The argument that states it is logical to proceed from an integrated program in the primary school to a separated program in the post-primary is a force of tradition. In launching a new program, where one begins should be less determined by educational ideals and more by where the best teachers and materials are available. When the Northern Nigeria Teacher Education Project (NNTEP) introduced the subject in 1964, it was to grade II teachers' colleges. The rationale declared it essential first to train the teachers for the primary school and then start the primary program itself. NNTEP completed its work in 1969. Soon thereafter other bodies became involved; but instead of building on the foundations already laid at the teacher education level, they decided to clear new ground at the primary school level. This shift in emphasis has created a situation in which teachers trained in the traditional geography and history are used to promote integrated social studies in the schools.

Social studies teaching puts a greater demand on teachers and school administrators than does the traditional approach. The teacher of social studies must be a curriculum-maker. In other words, he or she must have initiative and be trained in the art of inquiry.

At present, Nigeria's teachers are ill-equipped for this type of responsibility. They are themselves the products of a fragmented social science education. Throughout their years of training, they have had very little opportunity for original work. That is, they have not been trained in the processes of inquiry: locating sources, observing, gathering information, analysing facts, and formulating definitions.

Everyone involved with social studies in Nigeria is aware of this shortcoming in teacher skills. Accordingly, heavy emphasis is placed on orientation courses for teachers and on a supply of ready-made material for schools. Orientation courses are useful and the materials indispensable, but their ultimate worth is determined by the teachers who use them. It is acknowledged that to learn is easier than to unlearn. It is this problem that the orientation courses try to address. By and large, the teachers tend to teach as they have been taught. However, if overdone, orientation courses could make teachers develop negative attitudes to innovation. They may convey the implied message that one's original training has become inappropriate to current needs.

In sum, it is more logical to begin a new field of study which demands much initiative from the teacher, at the teachers' college level. These teachers would not regard the new program as an undermining force. Moreover, students having gone through the inquiry process during the training would obviously be more effective agents of change. They would have acquired the conviction and the confidence to influence the content of the programs they would teach.

The nature of social studies is a problem in itself. The fact that it has no body of knowledge of its own tends to relegate it to a low prestige, particularly among students in institutions of higher learning. Another problem is that of environment. The environment that surrounds the average school does not lend itself easily to study. Apart from the seasons, nothing else seems to change in the village. The child sees the same people at the same place doing the same thing almost every day of the year. Coupled with our tradition of making children accept things without question, this does not help children to develop inquiring minds. Moreover, the African tradition of "secrecy" and letting children discover things by themselves with age reduces the usefulness of community elders as resources.

Inadequate Resource Materials. Tradition would not pose a great problem if the world outside could be "brought" to the village. The general lack of materials acts as a great impediment to this end. Radio sets are few. Newspapers, journals, and magazines do not circulate to villages. Social studies lessons in such a situation cease to be "studies," as learning activities are limited to exposition, story-telling, and oral reports. Educational materials, where they exist, are too expensive for the regular school to purchase. Publishers in Nigeria do not give concessional rates to encourage the purchase and use of such materials in teaching.

Professional bodies, such as the Social Studies Association of Nigeria and the Nigerian Education Research Council, have drafted syllabuses, recommended methods, and suggested aids; but the lack of adequate funds has prevented sufficient materials from being produced.

Despite these problems, however, in the last decade considerable progress has been made. The facts that the State and Federal governments are spending money to support the development of social studies syllabuses and are financing in-service courses for teachers are indications of this progress and the growing awareness of the need for the integrated approach. These are encouraging signs. With determination and perseverance, the difficulties standing in the way will be surmounted in time. The magnitude of this progress can be realized if one remembers that it took the United States, the originator of integrated social studies, with huge material and human resources, a number of years to get social studies established as a recognised field of study. (Appendix is on pp. 72–75.)

NOTES

[1]Federal Ministry of Information, *Report on National Curriculum Conference Held September 8–12th, 1969*. Lagos, Nigeria, 1970.

[2]Aivetoro Comprehensive High School, Nigeria, *Social Studies for Nigerian School Teachers' Edition. Vols. I & II*. Lagos, Nigeria, 1968.

[3]P. E. Prokupek, *Geography and History Methods for Primary Schools*. Baraka Press Ltd., Nigeria, 1969.

[4]Nigeria Educational Research Council, *Guidelines on Primary School Curriculum: Report of the National Workshop on Primary Education April 26th–May 8th 1971*.

[5]Federal Ministry of Education, *Grade II Teachers' Syllabus*. Lagos, Nigeria, 1974.

[6]D. L. Dubey, V. O. Onyabe, and P. E. Prokupek. *Social Studies Methods for Nigerian Schools: Learning Activities*. OUP, 1978.

[7]Federal Ministry of Information, *National Policy on Education*. Lagos, Nigeria, 1977.

Appendix

Nigerian National Policy on Education*

Objectives for Primary Education
1. The inculcation of permanent literacy and numeracy, and the ability to communicate effectively.
2. The laying of a sound basis for scientific and reflective thinking.
3. Citizenship education as a basis for effective participation in and contribution to the life of society.
4. Character and moral training and the development of sound attitudes.
5. Developing in the child of the ability to adapt to his changing environment.
6. Giving the child opportunities for developing manipulative skills that will enable him to function effectively in the society within the limits of his capacity.
7. Providing basic tools for further educational advancement, including preparation for trades and crafts of the locality.

Objectives for Secondary Education
1. Provide an increasing number of primary school pupils with the opportunities for education of a higher quality irrespective of sex, or social, religious, and ethnic background.
2. Diversify its curriculum to cater to the differences in talents, opportunities, and roles passed by or open to students after their secondary school course.
3. Equip students to live effectively in our modern age of science and technology.
4. Develop and project Nigerian cultures, art, and languages as well as the world's cultural heritage.
5. Raise a generation of people who can think for themselves, respect the views and feelings of others, respect the dignity of labor, and appreciate those values specified under our broad national aims and lives as good citizens.
6. Foster Nigerian unity with an emphasis on the common ties that unite us in our diversity.
7. Inspire its students with a desire for achievement and self-improvement both at school and in later life.

Objectives for Teacher Education
1. To produce highly motivated, conscientious, and efficient classroom teachers for all levels of our education system.
2. To encourage further the spirit of inquiry and creativity in teachers.

---

*Federal Ministry of Education, *National Policy on Education,* 1977.

3. To help teachers fit into the social life of the community and society at large and to enhance their commitment to national objectives.
4. To provide teachers with the intellectual and professional background adequate for their assignment and to make them adaptable to any change, not only in the life of their country but in the wider world.
5. To enhance teachers' commitment to the teaching profession.

Objectives for Higher Education
1. The acquisition, development, and inculcation of the proper value-orientation for the survival of the individual and society.
2. The development of the intellectual capacities of individuals to understand and appreciate their environments.
3. The acquisition of both physical and intellectual skills which will enable individuals to develop into useful members of the community.
4. The acquisition of an objective view of the local and external environments.

Nigerian Social Studies Objectives

*Social Studies Objectives for Primary Education**
1. Children's self-confidence and initiative, based on an understanding of their own accomplishments, potentialities, and worth.
2. Their power of imagination and resourcefulness.
3. Their desire for knowledge and continued learning.
4. Their appreciation of the dignity of man and liberty.
5. Their sense of compassion for the less fortunate.
6. Their sense of respect for and tolerance of the opinions of others, even in disagreement.
7. Their willingness to accept necessary changes within a system of law and order deriving from the will of the people.
8. Such attitudes that are favorable to social, physical, cultural, and economic development which enable the children to participate in the life of the community and, when they leave school, to function as innovators and doers of good in society.
9. Social attitudes and values such as cooperation, participation, interdependence on others, openmindedness, honesty, integrity, trustworthiness, hard work, obedience, etc.
10. A spirit of national consciousness and patriotism through interest and involvement in our local, national, and world heritage.
11. The creation of their social awareness, critical judgment as well as constructive effective thinking.

*Social Studies Objectives for Post-Primary Education**
1. To make students aware of the problems of their country and of the world in general, and to appreciate the interdependence between peoples.

*Developed by the Nigeria Education Research Council.

2. To create an awareness and understanding of the evolving social and physical environment, its natural, man-made, cultural, and spiritual resources together with the rational use and conservation of these resources for development.
3. To develop in the students a positive attitude to citizenship and a desire in them to make a positive personal contribution to the creation of a united Nigeria.
4. To develop a capacity to learn and to acquire skills essential to the formation of a satisfactory professional life (i.e., a pride in a job and sound judgment).
5. To develop in the student an appreciation of his cultural heritage and a desire to preserve it.

These objectives are reflected in the content of the national syllabuses, the major themes of which are presented below:

Social Studies Syllabus for Nigerian Primary Schools
Primary 1: Growing Up at Home and in School
  (a) The child in the home
  (b) Living in school as a family
  (c) Our duties to the nation
  (d) Current affairs
Primary 2: Urban and Non-urban Community Living
  (a) Review of Primary One syllabus
  (b) Living in local community
  (c) Our duties to the nation
  (d) Using social services
  (e) Current affairs
Primary 3: Working and Living Together in Our Local Government Area
  (a) Review of Primary Two syllabus
  (b) Who our neighbors are
  (c) How our local government area is administered
  (d) What our people do
  (e) Nigeria as a nation
  (f) Using and paying for social services
  (g) Current affairs
Primary 4: Social, Political, and Industrial Development of our State
  (a) Review of Primary Three work
  (b) Knowing other people from the state
  (c) Administrative set-up
  (d) Great lives in our state
  (e) Where and why industries are located
  (f) Nigeria as a nation
  (g) Using and paying for social services
  (h) Current affairs
Primary 5: Unity in Diversity: Problems of Nation-building
  (a) Review of Primary Four syllabus
  (b) The story of Nigeria
  (c) How people live in other parts of Nigeria
  (d) Transportation and communication

(e) The wealth of Nigeria and recent development
(f) How Nigeria is governed
(g) Our role as a nation
(h) Nigeria as a nation
(i) Using and paying for social services
(j) Current affairs

Primary 6: People of Other Lands and Our Needs
(a) Review of the previous year's work
(b) How people live in other lands
(c) Foreigners in our midst
(d) Our relations with others
(e) The United Nations Organisation and its agencies
(f) Using and paying for social services
(g) Careers
(h) Nigeria as a nation—our flag and anthem
(i) Current affairs

Social Studies Syllabus for Nigerian Post-Primary Schools
Year 1
(a) Man in his environment
(b) Living together
(c) What we eat
(d) Farming
(e) Trades
(f) Means of transportation

Year 2
(a) The story of the early man
(b) Impact of science and technology on the society
(c) Family and kinship
(d) Political structure and organisation
(e) Economic structure and organisation
(f) Social and cultural systems

Year 3
(a) Living together in our community
(b) Living with other international neighbors
(c) Transportation and communication
(d) Public utilities
(e) Religious institutions
(f) The nature of social change

Year 4
(a) Socialization of man
(b) Unity and diversity of man
(c) Man's psychological needs
(d) Man's concern for others

Year 5
(a) Man's need for association and expression
(b) Man and his social rules and sanctions
(c) Man's use and conservation of resources
(d) Human resources
(e) Man's relation with his physical environment

Social Studies in England

Ray Derricott

WHAT DOES SOCIAL STUDIES MEAN IN ENGLAND?

The perspective presented in this chapter is English. This is because economic and internal political events in the United Kingdom in the last few years make it impossible to convey an adequate national perspective. The world oil crisis has ravaged the United Kingdom's economy, resulting in a difficult adjustment to massive inflation. The search for oil supplies has intensified. North Sea oil, which already has begun to flow to the refineries, promises only to provide a short lull in the economic battle. But to whom does the oil belong? Is it British or is it, as fervent Scottish Nationalists claim, Scotland's oil? The arrival of North Sea oil has accelerated interest in the transfer of political power from the one central government and parliament in London to separate assemblies for Scotland and Wales. Legislation to this end is now slowly proceeding through Parliament.

Scotland already has its own education system. Throughout the 1970s, the Scottish Centre for Social Subjects, with its headquarters in Glasgow, has been supporting Scottish teachers in their work by providing new ideas and materials. The decentralization of power, known as the devolution movement, is to some extent reflected in the increase of materials that focus on Scottish problems and cultural values. England and Wales operate under the same educational system; but, in Wales, Welsh language and cultural studies were a central part of the program of many schools long before the political movement towards devolution. In fact, it is doubtful whether the devolution issue has changed in any fundamental way what goes on in Welsh schools.

In Northern Ireland the situation is different. A decade of what is euphemistically called "the troubles" has eroded away many taken-for-granted aspects of community life. The effects on children have been the subject of much concern. Most schools attempt to carry on with their normal programs. In the areas worst affected, some teachers see life in school as a cocoon which deliberately isolates children from the surrounding conflict for part of each day. Some educators, working on the Cultural Studies Project at the New University of Ulster, have attempted to help teachers confront directly the problems of education in a divided society.

These broad sweeps of the pen cannot do justice to the nuances of British social studies. They are intended to indicate why this chapter presents only an English viewpoint and to suggest that the consequence of political fragmentation is a challenge to be faced by social studies education in the United Kingdom.

The presence of a devolution movement is not the only factor that makes the late 1970s an appropriate time to review the state of social studies education in the United Kingdom. A salient effect of the lack of economic growth and the escalation of inflation has been the need to curtail public spending. One of the first targets for such a curtailment was government spending on education. A fierce program of cuts over the last few years has reduced drastically both teacher supply and money available for resources in schools. In this forbidding economic climate, the education system has been called upon to make itself accountable. This accountability has been concentrated on the assessment of standards in the basic school subjects such as language and mathematics. However, it has been accompanied by a significant and persistent set of questions about what schools are achieving for their pupils in terms of social understanding. Much of this debate has echoed the discussion of the 1930s and 1940s about the kinds of citizens that schools were producing.

The Educational System in England

Before developing the perspective on social studies education, it is necessary to provide a brief background on the structure of the educational system in England and to comment on the examination system, which has a direct influence on what is taught.

Structure of the Education System. Although subsequent legislation has changed many of its detailed provisions, the Education Act of 1944 provides the legal basis for education in England and Wales. It defines primary education as operating to the age of eleven and secondary education as operating beyond that age. The 1944 Act introduced universal, free secondary education for all. Education according to age, ability, and aptitude is to be provided by Local Education Authorities (LEAs). For over twenty years, most LEAs interpreted the Act by providing a selective system of secondary education with 15–20% of pupils being allocated to selective grammar schools and the rest to secondary modern schools.[1] Research throughout the 1950s showed this system to be ineffective. It was a system of social rather than academic selection. Since the 1960s, an increasing number of LEAs have abolished selection altogether and provided an open admissions policy with respect to comprehensive secondary schooling. In 1978, almost 80% of the children attended comprehensive secondary schools until the school-leaving age of sixteen. Increasing numbers of students stay on until the age of eighteen to complete examinations for entry to higher education. These qualifications enable them to begin some form of professional or vocational training.

Examination System. The present examination system stems, in the main, from reform introduced in 1951. It provides for two main levels of examination for a General Certificate of Education (GCE). The Ordinary level of the GCE is usually taken at around fifteen or sixteen and the Advanced level at eighteen. Both the O and A-level GCE can be taken at later ages and is not limited to candidates attending school full-time.

The GCE, O-level examination is usually thought to be within the capabilities of students who are at the top 25% of the ability range. However, because every system of academic selection is bound to be imprecise and because some LEAs could provide grammar school places for only 8–10% of the population, many secondary modern schools began to offer a range of O-level courses. In 1965, to give some motivation to pupils not capable of taking O-level courses, a further, lower-level examination was introduced. This is called the Certificate of Secondary Education (CSE). It is organised by regional boards. It has led to a significant development in teacher-set and teacher-assessed examinations. The CSE is taken in the last year of schooling by sixteen-year-old students leaving school. Thus, in England there are three main levels of school examination: General Certificate of Education, with the Ordinary and Advanced levels and the Certificate of Secondary Education. This system provides examination opportunities and a nationally recognised indicator of level of attainment in schooling for about 75–80% of the school population. The remaining 20% are not thought capable of achieving even the lowest level of pass at CSE. Although this comprehensive system was designed to maximise equality of opportunity, it can still be viewed as hierarchical and elitist.

English Viewpoints on Social Studies: A Suggested Typology

While musing over how one could convey English ideas and attitudes about social studies to a mainly American readership, this author became involved in a workshop course at a Teachers' Centre. This workshop included primary, middle, and secondary school teachers. It considered ways in which liaison between schools could be improved, particularly in relation to assessment and record-keeping. The specialities of the member teachers ranged from mathematics, English, history, geography, and biology to religious education, French, physical education, and craft and design. The teachers were by no means a representative sample, but their responses to the question "What is meant by social studies in your school?" makes the first point. Some of the replies received are listed below:

> We don't do social studies. We do environmental studies and individual topic work. (Deputy head, primary school)

> We have an integrated course called social studies. It is mainly geography and history. . . . We try to give the children a view of how people in a community depend on each other. (Primary School teacher)

> We have a humanities scheme throughout the four years of the school. It incorporates history and geography, but we have increasingly been trying to use anthropological material as well as ideas from sociology and economics—but only at a very simple level. . . . (Middle School Deputy Head)

I'm concerned because in our school the first three years do environmental studies and social studies . . . but it doesn't include much history. . . . They can opt for history and geography in the fourth year (14+) but many of them have got out of the habit. Even the bright ones go for sociology and the "less able" go for community studies. (History specialist, comprehensive school)

Our local comprehensive school has a social education faculty that presumably takes care of social studies. . . . I don't know what he does but he's got a lot of staff involved in social education. . . . (Primary School Head teacher)

Even in a small and unrepresentative group such as the one used, there are almost as many views about social studies as there are teachers. Certainly, it is impossible to find a consensus on the definition of social studies. And in a system such as ours, which works hard at preserving what some people would call the myth of autonomy of the school, it is difficult, if not dangerous, to generalise. Nevertheless, against this background this author will try to make some sense of the English social studies scene.

The lack of consensus among teachers as to what constitutes social studies is, in major part, a reflection of their own education. Most teachers over the age of thirty are the products of selective grammar schools in which social studies did not appear in the curriculum. Viewed as low-status knowledge, social studies courses were the preserve of the secondary modern school. Even younger teachers, who have been educated through the comprehensive school system, will have experienced little social studies during their schooling. They would have been guided towards history and geography courses. These subjects are regarded as strong currency in the applications to colleges and universities. Economics and British constitution or government have been Advanced-level subjects for many years, but often have been seen as second option choices of much lower status than the traditional pre-university, sixth-form content of history, geography, and English literature.

Many of the British teachers trained since the early 1960s will have had a sociological perspective introduced into their studies of educational theory. However, few will have received any adequate and systematic professional preparation for the teaching of social studies. Some teachers, being prepared for work in upper primary, middle schools, and lower secondary schools (ages eight to thirteen, the middle years of schooling in England), will have undertaken work in integrated courses that may have included a social studies component. However, to generalise, it is believed that the situation in terms of teacher competency in social studies is very much as Lawton saw it in 1971. Reporting on the state of social studies with particular reference to the middle years of schooling he held that: "Social studies is an area which is of great interest and value to children . . . but at present teachers are not well equipped by their training to exploit their pupils' curiosity in this field."[2]

Recent work by Gleeson and Whitty[3] confirms the lack of consensus about social studies among teachers and includes some illuminating references to pupils' perceptions of social studies courses. These strongly suggest that the message about social studies has not been communicated with any clarity to the ultimate consumers—the pupils.

In England, there is no one clear and dominant tradition of social studies teaching. Instead, there is a wide variety of approaches, of which the main types are:

Type 1: *Social Studies* which are an amalgam of history and geography. This type is found mainly in primary (ages five to eleven) schools and often concentrates on local studies.

Type 2: *Civics Education.* The emphasis in these courses is on providing knowledge about the workings of local and national government. Attention is often focused also on the health, welfare, and general community services. A topic such as "law and order" would be tackled by examining the services provided by the police, but one would never ask critical questions about society and the control of behaviour. The major objectives of such courses are often expressed in terms of the development of *informed citizens.*

Type 3: *Social Education.* A recent national curriculum development project saw the aim of such courses as the provision of

an enabling process through which children will achieve a sense of identity with their community, become sensitive to its shortcomings and develop methods of participation in those activities needed for the solution of social problems.[4]

The emphasis here is on the development of self-reliance, social understanding, and other social skills such as empathy, through an *active* interest in community affairs.

Type 4: *Social Science Education.* An approach which uses the disciplines of the social sciences—anthropology, economics, politics, sociology—either separately or in combination, as resources in course planning. Courses of this kind emerged in the 1960s in response to the lack of rigour that often characterised old style social studies. Thus began the "new social studies" movement, the progress of which has been documented to the early 1970s with admirable clarity by Lawton and Dufour.[5] Initially, the movement was centered at the London University Institute of Education. An early article by one of the leaders of this movement, Charmian Cannon, suggested a guide to course planning which would help to avoid some of the weaknesses found in earlier social studies courses. Cannon advocated that:

1. The work must have a *well defined content* in order to avoid the diffuseness of earlier efforts.
2. Courses must contain ideas, concepts, and processes that encourage *academic rigour.*
3. Courses must have clearly thought-out aims and *be "conceived in less manipulative terms* than good citizenship or education for identification."[6]

John Stangl and students at the Stramongate County School in England explore the possibilities of reconstructing reality from clay, straw, and paper. Used with permission of Mr. Stangl, Cowern Elementary School, North St. Paul, Minnesota.

Courses of the type labelled Social Science Education developed during the 1960s, keeping Cannon's principles in mind and using the resources of anthropology, sociology, and, on occasion, economics. However, progress was slow because the curricula of English schools are extraordinarily difficult to penetrate with new ideas.

Rogers found that much of the innovative work in social studies was being carried out in isolation.[7] There appeared to be few networks through which like-minded innovators could be brought together. He also found that there was considerable teacher suspicion of the use of the social sciences in schools and, echoing the present author's own words, significant numbers of teachers believe that young children should be "protected" from, rather than introduced to, sensitive social issues.[8, 9] "Thinking" about social issues was seen to be the preserve of older adolescents.

In practice, many of the courses that emerged during the late 1960s and the early 1970s organised around social problems were designed for less able young school-leavers (fourteen to sixteen years old). These courses were rarely considered by the students able enough to take GCE, Ordinary and Advanced-level examinations. Such courses have been described as "diluted, unchallenging and insultingly condescending studies, often on the local environment, local social services, and social 'problems.' "[10] These courses are considered as Type 2 Civics Education courses.

Thus, despite the considerable skill, energy, and enthusiasm by the proponents of the new social studies movement, its development to 1968 had been slow. Since that time, the increasing influence of three factors has acted to change, to a considerable extent, the English social studies scene.

First, the publication of the Newsom Report,[11] with its advocacy of the raising of the school-leaving age from fifteen to sixteen and its appeal for an education "that makes sense" for average and below average pupils in the thirteen to sixteen age group, increased the urgency to develop courses that are "practical, realistic and vocational." Second, the Schools Council for Curriculum and Examinations, set up in 1964 as a central agency to support national curriculum development, and which places great stress on its claim to be teacher controlled, began to support regional and national projects in the areas of the humanities and social studies.[12]

A subordinate, and not often elaborated effect of the establishment of the Schools Council, was the impetus its activities gave to spreading the British version of the rational curriculum planning movement. The use of aims, objectives, and evaluation strategies in curriculum planning represents a new orthodoxy. The language of rational curriculum planning has permeated the planning documents produced by individual middle and comprehensive schools[13] and the published syllabi of many examination boards, particularly those of the Certificate of Secondary Education.[14]

This leads to the third factor. In England, one of the most effective ways of bringing about changes in curricula is to introduce new CSE, GCE, O and A-level examinations or to change existing examination syllabi. To this end, the sociologists have been particularly active and successful. These examinations are run by a number of separate boards. The Associated Examining Board and the Oxford Board have been examining O and A-level sociology since the middle 1960s. The Joint Matriculation Board (Manchester based) offered A-level sociology for the first time in 1976 and the London and Cambridge Boards have already entered this field. There is no doubt about the growing popularity of sociology as an A-level option. The examination syllabi of these Boards, in large measure, control the content and the teaching of sociology in the upper secondary schools.

In their recent analysis of this situation, Gleeson and Whitty show how the contents of examination syllabi at all levels tend to be the same, although the way each course is assessed may vary tremendously. They conclude that:

> Social studies is coming to be defined very much in the style of the O and A level syllabuses which were first developed during the 1960's. This consensual redefinition of social studies in terms of conventional sociology has taken place despite major changes in the nature of academic sociology in recent years and despite growing doubts about the extent to which such sociology can . . . help students to understand themselves as individuals and the society to which they belong.[15]

Table 1: Types of Social Studies Courses

Type of Social Studies	Age Group	Required or Optional	Sequential or Non-sequential	Integrated or Separate	Examination or Non-examination
Type 1 Social Studies	5–11	Required	Non-sequential	Integrated	Non-examination
Type 2 Civics Education	10–11	Required	Sequential	Integrated	Non-examination
Type 3 Social Education	13–16	Optional	Non-sequential	Integrated	Non-examination or teacher assessed C.S.E.
Type 4 Social Science Education	14–18	Optional	Sequential	Separate treatment	Examination G.C.E. O & A level

Thus the new social studies—that is, those courses designated as social science education, which developed as a reaction to the lack of academic rigour and structure—are now themselves being held in question. This author's perceptions of social studies in England are summarized above.

Type 1 Social Studies are most likely found in primary schools and are required for all children. Work is usually individual or group projects which are seen as part of an integrated program. Little or no attention is given to the systematic selection and sequencing of content. There are no external examinations involved.

Type 2 Civics Education courses are most frequently found in the middle schools as part of the required program. These courses emphasize the development of an informed citizen. The content is sequential; its focus is on the workings of the government and on community services. No external examination is given.

Type 3 Social Education courses are most likely found as an optional element in secondary comprehensive schools. These courses are often community-based. Work stems from a number of general questions asked about the local community. In planning such courses, the approach is "integrated" and "non-sequential." These courses are either non-examinable or are offered as a Mode 3, Certificate of Secondary Education. This means that the courses are devised by teachers in particular schools to meet the needs of their students. Assessment is moderated by the examinations board but is in the hands of the teachers.

Type 4 Social Science Education courses use the social science disciplines in course planning. These courses feature a well defined content with a sequential approach. They are most often found at the secondary level as an optional component. GCE examinations are given at both the O and A-levels.

WHAT IS THE RELATIONSHIP BETWEEN SOCIAL STUDIES AND CITIZENSHIP EDUCATION?

One can link the periodic emergence and decline of public concern about citizen education in the United Kingdom with recurring political and economic crises and with social change.

During the post-World War II period, the view generally expressed was that schools had a positive role to play in the development of citizenship. This was seen by the Norwood Committee as being best achieved by the adjustment in emphasis in the teaching of history and geography to include citizenship perspectives.[16] Historians and geographers were encouraged to develop social studies courses with an emphasis on child-centered, "active" learning through projects. These would be Type 1 courses as described above.

The period from 1951 saw the development and implementation of the O and A-level examination system. Social studies courses that retained their citizenship components became considered as low-status activities. The Crowther Report suggested that the curriculum at the fifteen to eighteen age level should contain "four strands":

> There is, first, the task of helping young workers, many of them of limited intelligence, *to find their way successfully about the adult world—to spend their money sensibly, to understand the many ways in which the welfare state touches their lives and can assist them, to see how its services are paid for and to play their part as useful citizens.* Secondly, there is the more difficult job of *helping them to define,* in a form which makes sense to them, *a standard of moral values by which they can live* after they have left the sheltered world of school and find themselves in novel situations where they desperately need guidance.[17]

In terms of citizen education, what the Crowther Report recommended for this age group the Newsom Report (1963) repeated for the average and below average pupils of thirteen to sixteen years. The Newsom Report favoured structured courses. However, it also urged that teaching should encourage critical thinking about the strengths and limitations of evidence and "an ability to enter imaginatively into other men's minds. What is to be cultivated here is psychological sensitivity and intuitive awareness rather than rational fact finding."

In England, however, citizenship education is sometimes viewed as outmoded, a suspect idea which often aims at manipulating students' values to fit the societal status quo. Nevertheless, there are signs that citizen education is both returning to the top of the agenda and is in the process of being redefined.

The Great Debate on Education

At the end of 1976, Prime Minister Callaghan initiated what has been called the Great Debate on educational standards. The Prime Minister was voicing public disquiet about the falling standards mainly in basic language and mathematics skills. Industry stated that schools did not understand its needs and were not producing the right calibre of entrants. The trade unions declared that schools did not provide young people with an understanding of industrial democracy. In this sense, the English people were told that as a nation they were politically and functionally illiterate.

The teaching profession responded to the criticism by producing a document which included an acknowledgment of the need for teacher accountability. Back in 1974, the Department of Education and Science had set up the Assessment of Performance Unit (APU) "to promote the development of methods of assessing and monitoring the achievement of children in school and to seek to identify the incidence of under achievement."[18]

The Great Debate has given further impetus and status to the work of the APU. Standards are being monitored and assessed in six areas, which include the area of personal and social development. What is emerging in the field of personal and social development is a redefinition of citizen education. Personal and social development is seen as at least the following:

(a) the student's understanding of himself or herself and of others;
(b) the student's moral development;
(c) the student's understanding of and attitude towards environmental issues (e.g., pollution, energy saving);
(d) the student's ability to make rational decisions about choice of career;
(e) the student's ability to make rational decisions as a consumer;
(f) the student's development of political understanding; and
(g) the student's understanding of religion and comparative religious beliefs.

The definition of personal and social development is wide; the tasks of assessing performance are immense. Some of the seven areas outlined above either are not taught *directly* in many schools or are not taught at all. Some areas are not taught to pupils of a particular ability or of a particular age. Will the activities of the APU eventually be interpreted as an indication of what *ought* to be included in the curriculum? If this is so, it will be a break from a long held English tradition that in matters related to the curriculum there is only minimal central direction.

The last point needs some elaboration. For example, present consumer education is a component in a minority of social studies courses. It is probably more evident in Social Education courses (Type 3) intended for young school-leavers. Many able pupils pursuing examinations will have no direct experience with consumer education. Similarly, political education is an option for that minority of students that chooses the appropriate GCE O and A-level courses. There has been a call by the current Secretary of State for Education Science for a more direct teaching of politics. Accordingly, there has been considerable debate about the susceptibilities of young people to political propaganda. Thus, the attempt of the APU to map out the field of personal and social development is introducing a redefined concept of citizen education which should support those teachers experimenting with Social Education courses (Type

3). It may even lead to a change of emphasis in Social Science Education courses (Type 4) so that they can become both "meaningful and critical."[19]

WHAT ARE THE MAJOR ISSUES IN THE SOCIAL STUDIES IN ENGLAND?

In considering the key problems that face social studies educators in England as the 1980s approach, many have ignored the universal and obvious needs for more money, teachers, and resources. The facts are that education in England is facing falling school enrollments. The biggest challenge will be to make more effective and professional use of what is already here.

Cultural Pluralism.

The debate on devolution highlights the traditional and cultural differences that exist *within* British society. The continued existence of a United Kingdom in its present form can no longer be taken for granted. Both the consequences of this and the special Scottish, Welsh, and English viewpoints on social issues need to be written into the social studies curriculum. British society needs to become less insular. Britain has been a member of the European Economic Community for several years, but the development of European attitudes and perspectives is missing from most social studies curricula, as is the development of world studies or global education. Movements for global education do exist, mostly supported by small bands of enthusiasts. However, they remain peripheral, low-status activities fighting for time and recognition in the mainstream curriculum.

Decentralized Decision-making.

The debate about devolution is a debate about decision-making: the call is for decentralization to move decision-making away from distant politicians and bureaucrats and closer to the people whose lives are affected. Parallel to this movement are calls for worker participation in the management of industry and increased lay participation in the management of schools. Participation is the key concept; but if it is to become more than a hollow, political slogan, the schools must prepare their students. They must give students the experience of participatory decision-making in school life and in community affairs.

Multiethnic Education.

Another issue that confronts the English social studies educator is providing a multiethnic education. Approximately six percent of the population of Britain is immigrant, non-European. Immigration of black and brown people, mainly from the West Indies, India, and Pakistan, is a phenomenon of the past twenty years. Legal and institutional reaction to this influx has been slow. Because these immigrants have concentrated in certain urban areas, there has been a tendency to treat the need for multiethnic education as being special to those areas and not for the rest of the country. Most courses and the attendant materials have a strong Anglo-Saxon bias. In general, the social studies teacher avoids handling sensitive topics such as relations between the different ethnic groups.[20] The recent increase in the activities of the racist National Front party has brought questions from Members of Parliament about what the schools are achieving in relation to the development of liberal-democratic views towards race relations. One hopes that this concern can be translated into support for innovations in multiracial education in the schools.

These, then, are the key problems facing the social studies educator in England. It should be noted that the word *citizenship* is absent in most of this discussion. Even though what is being explored fits very neatly under this label, today's educators remain skeptical of using this term.

NOTES

[1]Of course, Public Schools still exist. What we in Britain call Public Schools are really privately run, totally autonomous schools for fee-paying students. These cater to around one per cent of the school population. Some of the most famous are Eton, Harrow, Winchester, and Rugby.

[2]D. Lawton, J. Campbell, and V. Burkitt, "Schools Council Working Paper 39," *Social Studies 8–13*. London: Evans-Methuen, 1971.

[3]D. Gleeson and G. Whitty, *Developments in Social Studies Teaching.* London: Open Books, 1976.

[4]J. Rennie, E. A. Lunzer, and W. T. Williams, "Schools Council Working Paper 51," *Social Education: An Experiment in Four Secondary Schools.* London: Evans-Methuen, 1976.

[5]D. Lawton and B. Dufour, *The New Social Studies.* 2nd Edition, London: Heinemann, 1976.

[6]C. Cannon, "Social Studies in the Secondary School," *Educational Review.* (Birmingham University) 17:1 (November) 1964.

[7]V. Rogers, *The Social Studies in English Education.* London: Heinemann, 1968.

[8]R. Derricott, et al. *Themes in Outline.* London: Collins, ESL, Bristol, 1971.

[9]W. A. L. Blyth and R. Derricott, et al. *Curriculum Planning in History, Geography and Social Science.* London: Collins, ESL, Bristol, 1976.

[10]Lawton and Dufour, *op. cit.,* p. 15.

[11]Ministry of Education, *Half Our Future.* (Newsom Report). London: H. M. S. O., 1963.

[12]Two of the early ones were the North West Curriculum Development Project and the Humanities Curriculum Project.

[13]W. A. L. Blyth and R. Derricott, *The Social Significance of Middle Schools.* London: Batsford, 1977.

[14]Each C.S.E. Board issues guidelines for teachers planning their own Mode 3 courses, couched in the language of rational curriculum planning.

[15]Gleeson and Whitty, *op. cit.,* pp. 30–31.

[16]Ministry of Education, *Curriculum and Examinations in Secondary Schools.* (Norwood Report). London: H. M. S. O., 1943.

[17]Ministry of Education, *15 to 18.* (The Crowther Report). London: H. M. S. O., 1959, p. 274.

[18]D. T. E. Marjoram, "What the APU Hopes to Achieve," *T.E.S.,* 1977.

[19]Gleeson and Whitty, *op. cit.,* p. 111.

[20]D. Hill, *Teaching in Multiracial Schools: A Guidebook.* London: Methuen, 1976.

Social Studies in the United States: Global Challenges

Jan L. Tucker

In the first chapter, Howard Mehlinger raised the question, "What is the value to Americans of understanding social studies as it exists in other nations?" One of the major benefits is the insight which we can gain about ourselves. It's a bit like traveling abroad or living in another culture—the more we learn about others, the more sensitive we become to the underlying patterns of life at home.[1]

At the very least, the penetrating contributions of Ray Derricott, Annette Kuhn, Absorn Meesing, Jiro Nagai, and Vincent Onyabe open our eyes to the fact that the growth and development of social studies in other nations are often associated with the cutting issues of social, political, and economic life. In many other nations, to a greater or lesser degree, social studies is a corollary of the global revolution of rising political, economic, and social expectations that has characterized much of the twentieth century. As noted in earlier chapters, social studies has been imported by other nations from the United States (or exported by the United States, if you prefer) as a means to achieve social change and political reform.

The particular nature of this change and reform has varied from one nation to another. In Nigeria, for example, social studies has been introduced with the goal of breaking down regional, ethnic, and religious loyalties and building national unity. On the other hand, social studies in West Germany has been employed to help mitigate the consequences of nationalism run amuck. The common theme, however, in both instances is that social studies is viewed as an educational tool designed to break the cake of custom.

Social studies in the United States was envisioned in this vigorous fashion by many who helped lay its foundations during the period between the two world wars. But today, social studies appears to lie in the eddies, and not the mainstream, of American life. American social studies in the 1970s has turned sharply away from the reflective thinking, social issues, inquiry, and interdisciplinary approaches—all of which were hallmarks of a social studies that looked to the future and to the possibility of helping shape a new social order.

The specific intent of this, the final chapter, is to invite the reader to contemplate whether social studies in the United States ought once again to be viewed as an instrument of social change and reconstruction. If there are reasons to so conceive social studies, then what are the inherent issues which must be faced? The inquiry is organized around two questions. They are:

1. What are the political, economic, and social implications of the global revolution of rising expectations?
2. What challenges does the global revolution of rising expectations hold for social studies in the United States?

What Are the Implications of the Global Revolution of Rising Expectations?

Exponential growth, constantly doubling, is one of the hallmarks of the last half of the twentieth century. Lester Brown uses the metaphor of the pond that starts with one lily pad. With the lily pads doubling in number every day, in twenty-nine days of exponential growth the pond is half-filled with lily pads. He poses the question: How many more days will it take for the pond to be completely filled with lily pads? The answer, of course, is *one* more day. Brown suggests that Earth, like the pond, is on the brink of the thirtieth day.[3]

Lee F. Anderson writes of the J-curve growth phenomenon, another perspective on exponential growth.[4] 1, 2, 4, 8, 16, 32, 64, . . . etc. Plotted on a graph, these numbers take the form of the capital letter J. According to Professor Anderson, ours is the century of the J-curve. During this century, we have experienced growth probably unparalleled in human history. We can expect more of the same in the foreseeable future. In almost every important facet of human affairs, we can identify the J-curve phenomenon: world population growth, increase in the killing radius of weapons, consumption of resources, number of war-related deaths, speed of communication, and consumption of synthetic products.

Exponential growth has become one of the most significant events in human history. Professor Anderson writes:

Question: Where, my child, do you live in time?
Answer: I live around the bend of many J-curves.[5]

The Global Revolution of Rising Expectations as a J-Curve Phenomenon. Almost two decades ago, Robert Heilbroner brought to our attention that a global revolution of rising human expectations—the hope for a better material, political, and spiritual life—was well underway and represented a significant event in human history.[6] Indeed, this revolution of rising expectations, or the Great Ascent, as Heilbroner called it, is now considered as one of the first clearly recognizable examples of the J-curve phenomenon. Thus, the rapid increase in human aspirations during the twentieth century may be conceived in terms of exponential growth. Heilbroner described its magnitude, its attractions, and its importance for the future:

Figure 1. World Population Growth

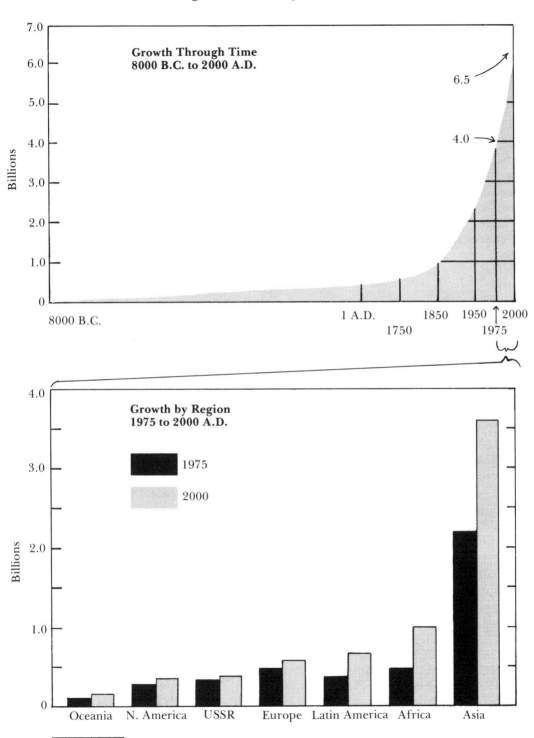

Courtesy of the Population Reference Bureau, 1337 Connecticut Ave., N.W., Washington, D.C.

It is not mere rhetoric to speak of this Great Ascent as the first real act of world history. Certainly in size and scope it towers over any previous enterprise . . . . For over one hundred nations, economic development means a chance to become a national entity, to live in the chronicle of recorded events. For over two billion human beings, it means something at once humbler and infinitely more important: the chance to become a personal entity, simply to live. And over and beyond this immense impact of development on the lives which are being led today looms its incalculably larger impact on the lives to be led tomorrow.[7]

The revolution of rising expectations is without precedent. It is global in scope. It will generate changes which now are only perceived dimly, but which for the future will pose enormous challenges, especially for the developed nations of the world—and for social studies educators who represent the developed nations.

Consequences of the Revolution of Rising Expectations. During the two decades since Heilbroner collected and synthesized the material for his book, *The Great Ascent: The Struggle for Economic Development in Our Time,* events have confirmed his major thesis that, indeed, the vision of a better life is one of the most powerful motivating global forces of the twentieth century. While the gap between rich and poor nations continues to exist, and is viewed by some as a problem even more serious than before,[8] the modernization process has spread around the globe and has engendered some remarkable successes, perhaps most notably in Japan.

Edwin Reischauer argues that the modernization breakthrough in Japan is a convincing indicator that the achievement of a better material life is not the sole province of the Western world.[9] Today, Japan serves as a prototype demonstrating that modernization is not only an aspiration of global magnitude, but also that it can become a global reality. Within a few decades, the dream may be achieved in other nations, such as Nigeria, Iran, Brazil, Mexico, and the People's Republic of China.

Any doubts that remained about the power wielded by the revolution of human expectations were considerably diminished by China's recently announced intention to modernize by the year 2000. In 1978, a billboard in Shanghai read "Take advantage of every minute, every second, to race to the year 2000." This slogan represents the quintessence of this revolution and stands as a global symbol of the twentieth century.

The global revolution of rising expectations is more than merely an elevation of the material standard of living. Attendant to the improved physical well-being are increases in political, economic, and social freedoms.

The most widely accepted expression of these fundamental freedoms is found in the Universal Declaration of Human Rights, adopted and proclaimed by the United Nations General Assembly on December 10, 1948. The heart of the Declaration is contained in its first Article, which reads, "All human beings are born free and equal in dignity and rights. They are endowed with reason and conscience and should act towards one another in a spirit of brotherhood." The Universal Declaration of Human Rights, together with the United Nations Charter, and the related international covenants, conventions, and declarations, constitute

争分夺秒 奔向2000！

A 1978 billboard in Shanghai declared, "Take advantage of every minute, every second, to race to the year 2000."

what has become known as the International Bill of Rights and comprise an important statement in the literature describing the revolution of rising expectations.[10]

The temporal, spatial, and moral dimensions that comprise the revolution of rising expectations have acted to set loose global forces which together will change the face of world relationships. It is in the context of this change that social studies in the United States may face its toughest challenge, an issue which we will return to later. But first, two of these global forces will be introduced and briefly examined.

Cultural Parity. Initially, in Northern Europe and the United States, and later elsewhere in the Western world, the revolution of rising expectations has been accompanied, in general, by a parallel belief of cultural superiority. It was taken for granted in the West that modernization and cultural dominance went hand-in-hand and that both were today, and would remain tomorrow, the special property of the early industrial nations. Today, as modernization spreads over the globe, this assumption is being challenged.

The UNESCO Conference on Cultural Parity, being planned for 1982, symbolizes the fact of a Western world being forced to leave behind the anachronistic attitude of "cultural disdain" and face up to the reality that the world of the twenty-first century is not being made over in the Western image. Even today's technological outcomes attributed to the revolution of rising expectations in probability will differ from those that would be familiar to the West. For example, Japan has managed to avoid the worst aspects of labor-management conflict by embodying the concept of a corporation into the traditional Japanese ideas of family responsibility.

Once a Japanese worker is hired into a company, he or she becomes "family" and is taken care of for life. Japanese corporations take seriously their social responsibility to develop human resources and consider it a condition necessary to producing quality products.

A recent policy that manifests the emerging cultural parity concept is the American position on the mass media resolution adopted at the 1978 UNESCO General Conference in Paris. The United States had three options: (1) to fight against any declaration on mass media in 1978; (2) to fight to the bitter end for a full-blown freedom of information declaration; or (3) to negotiate a consensus declaration that sacrificed as little as possible on freedom of information and, at the same time, gave credence to the position of Third World nations which preferred more governmental control of the mass media. The United States delegation chose to follow the third strategy and, after hard negotiation, helped forge the consensus Declaration on the Mass Media. The significance of this agreement is that, early in the negotiation, the United States decided to accept the idea of cultural parity in an international forum and worked for consensus.[11]

The United States is entering a new era of international decision-making and cannot afford either to be dogmatic on policy matters or disdainful of other cultures. Cultural parity, consensus assumptions, and multinational participation are very likely to become the basic ingredients of international decision-making.

Finite Resources. During the 1970s, it has become clear that the resources of Earth, especially fossil fuels, are in danger of being depleted if present trends of population growth and consumption come anywhere close to their predicted growth rates. For example, even with the discovery of new oil fields in Mexico and China, severe shortages of petroleum are expected to appear within the next decade. The global revolution of rising expectations is predicated on the assumption that available resources, especially energy resources, will stay apace with increasing demand.

A dilemma has developed: rising expectations versus finite resources. Rising expectations represent perhaps the most powerful burst of optimism in the twentieth century. The recent recognition that resources are finite represents an equally powerful realization of the limits to rising expectations. The consequences of the collision between the dream and the reality are yet to unfold.

Robert Heilbroner warns, "No developing country has fully confronted the implications of becoming a 'modern' nation-state whose industrial development must be severely limited . . . ."[12] He is pessimistic about the capacity of peoples and nations to negotiate successfully the challenges which lie ahead. He writes:

> . . . In all likelihood we must brace ourselves for the consequences . . . the risk of "wars of redistribution" or of "pre-emptive seizure," the rise of social tensions in the industrialized nations over the division of an ever more slow-growing or even diminishing product, and the prospect of a far more coercive exercise of national power as the means by which we will attempt to bring these disruptive processes under control.

From that period of harsh adjustment, I can see no realistic escape. . . . If, then, by the question, "Is there hope for man?" we ask whether it is possible to meet the challenges of the future without the payment of a fearful price, the answer must be: No, there is no such hope.[13]

In summary, the global revolution of rising expectations contains both hope and despair. The hope springs mainly from within the developing nations where the majority of people are striving to attain a minimal level of physical and psychological security. Typically, the despair emanates from those in the already industrialized nations who see an inevitable clash between modernization and the reality of finite resources, and who may also believe that the only conceivable solutions to this dilemma, short of wars of extermination, will destroy the political, social, and cultural freedoms known in the industrialized nations of the West.

For American social studies educators, the dilemma of modernization versus finite resources raises agonizing questions.

What Challenges Does the Global Revolution of Rising Expectations Hold for Social Studies in the United States?

On which horn of the emerging dilemma shall social studies in the United States choose to be caught? Shall social studies choose to foster the precepts and concepts of the now burgeoning revolution of rising expectations, thereby helping to build a new social order conceived on a global scale. Or shall it choose to emphasize the realities of finite resources, thereby potentially allying itself with the more conservative voices, whose most strident defenders would have the United States adopt a "lifeboat" philosophy—meaning that only those who are fortunate enough to be in the lifeboat already should be saved because it is impossible to save the others? Either choice involves risks.

Dare the Social Studies Help To Build a New Social Order? In 1932, George S. Counts, Professor of Education, Teachers College, Columbia University, published a pamphlet entitled *Dare the Schools Build a New Social Order?*[14] The challenge was issued to steer American educators toward the idea of using schools for the reconstruction of society. Counts was also a member of the American Historical Association's Commission on the Social Studies in the Schools, which included among its sixteen-person membership such notables as Charles A. Beard, Avery O. Craven, Carlton J. H. Hayes, Ernest Horn, Henry Johnson, Charles E. Merriam, and Jesse Newlon. Counts himself wrote one of the Commission's volumes, *The Social Foundations of American Education.* The seventeen volumes published by the AHA Commission on the Social Studies in the Schools are considered to be key contributions to the larger progressive education movement.[15]

The question of the role of schooling in social reconstruction was a corollary of a larger intellectual ferment of the 1930s which concerned the social role of organized knowledge.[16] Given the explosion of knowledge in almost every field of inquiry, and the deteriorating economic, social, and political conditions of the times, scholars were perplexed about the role of the organized disciplines. One form of the argument resided in the issues of whether knowledge was better offered within the discipline specializations or whether it was better integrated and synthesized. A second issue was knowledge for its own sake versus knowledge applied to the solution of social problems. The AHA Commission on Social Studies in the Schools came down solidly for both the integration and application of scholarly disciplines. By the mid-1930s, the intellectual leadership of the social studies indeed appeared to believe that education should be used to create a new social order and that social studies ought to play a leading role.

Intellectual ferment was one thing; what was happening in the schools was another. The Counts' agenda was never adopted; in fact, not many classroom teachers read it in the first place.[17] In 1939, Robert S. Lynd published *Knowledge for What?*[18] This was perhaps the last strong plea, prior to the Second World War, for the social application of the social sciences.

World War II and its Cold War aftermath created a new era. Progressive education and its goal of education for social reconstruction could not survive the forbidding intellectual climate. Indeed, progressive education was viewed in some circles as the major culprit for the ills of American education in the 1950s. The era came to a close when the Progressive Education Association disbanded in 1955.[19]

Today, the few remaining second-generation social reconstructionists are disillusioned and some now question the original assumptions which undergirded the ferment of the 1920s and 1930s and, in turn, provided the intellectual impulse for their own social studies curriculum development work in the 1960s. For example, Donald Oliver, principal architect of the Harvard Project Social Studies, now contends that the hopes of early social reconstructionists, like Harold Rugg, were naive and that their belief in formal schooling as the vanguard of social reform is not supported by the facts.[20]

According to Oliver, the good life in a secular democratic state is defined by standards of gross national product, employment and health statistics, and, generally, a counting up of goods and services. He suggests that this materialistic belief system may so fragment life that people lose touch with the "world whole, as a single moral order with interrelated values and assumptions." It is this quest for a "world whole" that provides the spark that legitimates the question, "Dare the Social Studies Help To Build a New Social Order?"

The Emerging Global Context for American Social Studies. Donald Oliver's plea for a "world whole" represents a clear-cut example of the increasing realization by an expanding range of American social studies educators that a global context is a much needed dimension for rethinking the purposes and the practices of social studies education in the United States. Some social studies educators may disagree with Oliver on whether the concept of "world whole" should be defined as a "single moral order." But such disagreements should not obscure that the need for holistic structures has been identified and that the intellectual search process is underway.

The major theme unifying this new inquiry has two aspects: (1) social studies education, as now conceived in the United States, is inadequate to prepare our youth for the challenges and the opportunities of the emerging global age; and (2) social studies needs a global perspective infused into its traditional and ongoing function of citizenship education.

Global trends, such as growing economic interdependence, an increasing awareness of our common origins, and a shared sense of human destiny, are challenging the thinking of social studies educators in the United States. There is an increasing recognition that our nation-centered citizen education needs to be reconstructed to better fit a world where an ever-growing number of problems are beyond the capacity of individual nations to resolve. It is likely that this trend will be welcomed by other nations and cultures that are concerned that citizens of the United States are ill-informed about world politics and that are apprehensive about such ignorance, especially in a powerful democratic nation where public opinion can sway foreign policy decisions.[21]

Social studies education in the United States reconceived within the emerging global context will require universal, global concepts to achieve the "world whole" sought by Oliver. In this regard, Lee Anderson has identified the J-curve, as noted earlier.[22] James Becker has suggested the concept of human inclusiveness, in part, the relative lack of concern of the national origins of ideas.[23] Robert Leestma calls for a development of the values of intergenerational stewardship—the capacity of one generation to make policy decisions based on the welfare of future generations.[24] Thomas Buergenthal and Judith Torney urge that a greater attention be devoted to the concept of international human rights.[25] Robert Johns argues that the notion of "man-in-dialogue" is important to an understanding of global processes.[26] Robert Hanvey has described several dimensions required to achieve a global perspective.[27]

Taken in the aggregate, these formulations represent a substantial effort among American social studies educators to develop an enriched new configuration of social studies based upon a global perspective. As citizenship education is reconstructed for the twenty-first century, the task of social studies in the United States is to organize curriculum materials and instructional activities so that students may have more opportunities to gain a global perspective and to learn why to do so is in their self-interest. A momentum is developing; rarely now does one find strong support at the cutting edge for nation-centered citizenship education.

The Challenge. Education for a global perspective is education conceived as an agent for social change and reconstruction. Any decision to incorporate a global perspective into the social studies curriculum, however, will be followed in a few years by the issue of *which* particular perspective should be adopted. It is naive to assume that only one global perspective will emerge. Choices will be made. Conceivably, social studies in the United States (*qua* global education and social reconstruction) could follow one of at least two directions. One direction is consistent with the worldwide revolution of rising human expectations and supports the fundamental tenets of improved physical, psychological, and moral life for all of Earth's peoples and nations. Another direction, based upon the assumptions of finite resources, could conceivably take a hard line toward the poor nations and the poor within the industrialized nations. The pressure for social studies to choose the latter may well become even more compelling as events in the world run counter to national interests as perceived by the majority of citizens.

Education for a global perspective cannot be entered into lightly in a nation where historically attitudes toward the rest of the world have often been negative and isolationist. Social studies educators in the United States who have positive attitudes toward education for a global perspective must be sensitive to these realities and to the consequences of the potential range of future choices within education for a global perspective. In the final analysis, social studies education *qua* social reconstruction will be judged on the particulars, not the generalities, of global education.

Summary and Conclusion

With a variation in degree, the authors from other nations—Derricott, Kuhn, Meesing, Nagai, and Onyabe—view social studies in their respective nations as a force for social reconstruction. As such, social studies in other nations in the late 1970s is a corollary of the global revolution of rising expectations and is reminiscent of the earlier progressive education movement in the United States. A curious paradox exists. At the very time that social studies *qua* social reconstruction is being introduced in other nations, its assumptions based upon the model of the secular democratic state are being challenged in the United States by some of the very leaders who espoused it most vigorously during the 1960s.

As Howard Mehlinger pointed out in the first chapter, one of the dramatic realizations that comes with learning more about social studies in other nations is that social studies no longer remains the exclusive province of Americans. Consequently, no longer do Americans alone decide whether social studies can or should be conceived as an instrument to help build a new social order. Despite what American educators may decide is the correct approach to social studies within the United States, if educators abroad determine a different course for social studies in their respective nations, those in the United States must take that difference into serious account.

In the past two decades, as a parallel to the revolution of rising expectations, American educators have witnessed a globalization of the social studies and can no longer afford to be provincial and exclusively nation-centered about their profession. The point here is to suggest that while other nations may have much to learn from the United States about social studies, the United States may have as much to gain from other nations. The exchange will enrich the social studies, an emerging transnational profession.

NOTES

[1]The overarching purpose of this final chapter is to identify the most fundamental implications for social studies in the United States which can be gleaned by an analysis of social studies in other nations. Conceivably, the reader may bring a different analytic framework to bear on the data contained in the earlier chapters and, consequently, will draw different conclusions. If so, a rewarding long-range result of learning about social studies in other nations is that the process will enrich our understanding of social studies as it is still emerging in the United States.

[2]The concept of the global revolution of rising expectations is important to social studies in two ways. The more conventional relationship is employing the concept as content to be taught in social studies classrooms. The second relationship, and the one used in this chapter, is utilizing the concept as a tool for analyzing social studies as a subject area in the curriculum. In this latter sense the concept is useful as part of the study of the foundations of social studies.

[3]Lester R. Brown, *The Twenty-Ninth Day*. New York: W.W. Norton and Company, 1978.

[4]Lee F. Anderson, *Schooling and Citizenship in a Global Age: An Exploration of the Meaning and Significance of Global Education*. Bloomington, Indiana: Mid-America Program for Global Perspectives in Education, Social Studies Development Center, Indiana University, 1979.

[5]*Ibid.*, p. 34.

[6]Robert L. Heilbroner, *The Struggle for Economic Development in Our Time*. New York: Harper and Row, Publishers, 1963.

[7]*Ibid.*, pp. 9–10.

[8]Barbara Ward, *The Home of Man*. New York: W.W. Norton and Company, Incorporated, 1976, pp. 258–268.

[9]Edwin O. Reischauer, *Toward the 21st Century: Education for a Changing World*. New York: Vintage Books, 1974.

[10]Thomas Buergenthal and Judith V. Torney, *International Human Rights and International Education*. Washington, D.C.: U.S. National Commission for UNESCO, Department of State, 1976 (available from Superintendent of Documents, U.S. Government Printing Office).

[11]This discussion regarding the 1978 UNESCO General Conference is based upon the author's notes taken at the December 1978 meeting of the U.S. National Commission for UNESCO, Washington, D.C., 1978.

[12]Robert L. Heilbroner, *An Inquiry into the Human Prospect*. New York: W.W. Norton, Incorporated, 1974, p. 131.

[13]*Ibid.*, pp. 135–136.

[14]George S. Counts, *Dare the Schools Build a New Social Order?* New York, 1932.

[15]Lawrence A. Cremin, *The Transformation of the School: Progressivism in American Education, 1876–1957*. New York: Vintage Books, 1961, p. 259.

[16]R. Freeman Butts and Lawrence A. Cremin, *A History of Education in American Culture*. New York: Holt, Rinehart and Winston, 1953, p. 508.

[17]Cremin, *op.cit.*, p. 264.

[18]Robert S. Lynd, *Knowledge for What?* Princeton: Princeton University Press, 1939.

[19]Cremin, *op.cit.*, p. 270.

[20]Donald W. Oliver, "Reflections on Peter Carbone's *The Social and Educational Thought of Harold Rugg*," *Social Education* 42:7 (November-December 1978) pp. 593–597.

[21]"What Should Be Known of International Politics in the U.S.?" Editorial, *Diario Las Americas*, Miami, Florida, January 10, 1979.

[22]Anderson, *op.cit.*

[23]James M. Becker, *Education for a Global Society*. Bloomington, Indiana: Phi Delta Kappa, 1973.

[24]Robert Leestma, "Global Education," *American Education*, June 1978, pp. 6–13.

[25]Buergenthal and Torney, *op.cit.*

[26]Robert W. Johns, "Man-in-Dialogue: An Image for Global-Minded Citizenship," *Theory and Research in Social Education* 6:2 (June 1978) pp. 1–25.

[27]Robert G. Hanvey, *An Attainable Global Perspective*, New York: Center for Global Perspectives (originally published by the Center for War/Peace Studies), N.D.

Index

Book design and production by Joseph Perez
Cover design by Bill Caldwell
Typography by Byrd PrePress
Printing and binding by Waverly Press